THE LIVING END

THE LIVING END

CHARLES CALDWELL RYRIE

Fleming H. Revell Company
Old Tappan, New Jersey

Scripture quotations identified KJV are from the King James Version of the Bible.

Scripture quotations identified NIV are from the NEW INTERNATIONAL VERSION. Copyright © 1973 by New York Bible Society International and are used by permission.

Scripture quotations identified NAS are from the New American Standard Bible, Copyright © THE LOCKMAN FOUNDATION 1960, 1962, 1963, 1968, 1971, 1972, 1973 and are used by permission.

Scripture quotations not otherwise identified are the author's own translation.

Library of Congress Cataloging in Publication Data
Ryrie, Charles Caldwell, date
  The living end.

  1. Bible—Prophecies. I. Title.
BS647.2.R93   236   76–4772
ISBN 0–8007–0799–0

Contents

THE LIVING END

1

No Recession for Prophets

An execution is always an ugly procedure.

The ancient Hebrews employed one of the ugliest: stoning.

Stripped naked with hands bound, the victim was paraded out of town and placed on a scaffold about nine feet high. The first official witness to the crime then roughly pushed him off the scaffold or, if there was no scaffold, into a hollowed-out depression in the ground. The victim might well hope that the fall would be fatal. But if not, the second official witness dropped a large stone on his head or chest. Bystanders then pelted the dying man with stones.

Even in death, insult was heaped on the dead person. The corpse was buried in a special place along with the stone which inflicted the fatal blow, and no mourning ceremony was permitted.

Unlike modern mob lynchings, the ancient practice of stoning was carefully regulated. On the basis of the testimony of witnesses, the case was tried before a judge, and the presence of the witnesses at the execution added solemnity to the proceedings. The law allowed for the last-minute appearance of new evidence in favor of the condemned.

Jesus was threatened with stoning several times; Stephen, the first Christian martyr, was executed that way; the apostle Paul experienced it but survived. Jesus berated those who stoned God's true prophets (Matthew 23:37).

But false prophets had to be stoned. The Law commanded it.

> But that prophet or that dreamer of dreams shall be put to death, because he has counseled rebellion against the Lord your God. . . . You shall stone him with stones so that he dies.
>
> Deuteronomy 13:5, 10

Prophecy was a risky business in ancient times! Today it is big business—and not nearly so risky.

Profits for Prophets

Every day millions read their horoscope in the newspaper expecting to discover what will happen to them that day. Millions of dollars are spent annually on astrology packets, fortune-tellers, and mediums. Lecture tours by self-proclaimed prophets and prophetesses reap huge profits. Sometimes these prophecies are couched in terms general enough that anyone could find a fulfillment in them. At other times they are specific but projected far into the future, so that by the time the events are supposed to happen, most people have forgotten what was predicted. And yet some very specific prophecies have had strikingly accurate fulfillments.

You Bet Your Life

But what modern prophet would be willing to stake his life on the truth of his claims? Do you know any? For that matter, do you know any medium, astrologer, prophet, or fortune-teller whose predictions have been correct 100 percent of the time? That's unreasonable, you say. Not at all. That's the norm for a true prophet! Prophets stay in business today only because their followers allow them to function at subnormal standards. If we required 100 percent accuracy, the prophecy boom would utterly collapse.

But there have been prophets who were willing to stake their lives on the truth of their predictions. And they lived long enough ago that we can easily test the accuracy of their predictions.

I am referring to the prophets of the Bible—men like Moses, Elijah, Isaiah, Jeremiah, Micah, Zechariah, Jesus, Paul, and many more. As spokesmen for God they commented on contemporary life from God's viewpoint, and at times they would forecast the future. Since many of their predictions have been fulfilled we can easily test the reliability of their predictions, and we can apply our findings to that portion of their prophetic work which has not yet had time for fulfillment, keeping in mind their unique batting averages in previous situations.

Put It in Writing

Have you ever played that game where the first person in a circle whispers a message to the second, the second to the third, and so on around the room? Then the last person tells everybody what he heard. Usually there is little resemblance to the original message. But if the same message were written down by the first person and simply passed around the circle, then of course the last person would receive the original message ungarbled and in its original wording.

Fortunately, the prophets of the Bible wrote out many of their messages. So in order to check the reliability of their predictions, we don't have to depend on hearsay. We can check the written records.

But can we trust the Bible? Many prophets wrote out their own messages, but these original writings have been lost. Many copies exist, however, which scholars study and compare in order to try to determine what the originals were. For example, there exist today more than five thousand copies in Greek of parts of the New Testament, more than eight thousand copies in Latin, and a thousand other copies in other languages. Compare this with the dearth of copies we have for other important books. There exist only nine or ten good copies of Caesar's *Commentaries on the Gallic War.* The *History* of Thucydides we have reconstructed from only eight manuscripts!

Copies of the Old Testament are much less plentiful, but there's a good reason for this. The copies of sacred writings were so highly regarded by the Jewish people that, when worn out from long use, they were buried in sacred ground as a mark of respect. Of course, a new copy was made before the old one was buried.

No Xerox in Those Days

Such copying was done with greater care than you can imagine. In order to prevent any error slipping into the new copy, the scribe carefully counted the number of letters and words on each page to be sure that every letter got into the new copy. He even located the middle letter on each page and in each book of the worn-out copy, then did the same with the new copy to double-check its accuracy. Think of doing that with the page you are reading now, and then imagine the painstaking care involved in doing it with entire books of the Bible.

There's no doubt about it—when we examine copies of what those ancient prophets wrote, we can safely say that we are looking at their original words.

Some Test Cases

Unlike much that passes for prophecy today, Bible prophecies in both the Old and New Testament were delivered not as groping generalizations or mystical musings but as detailed descriptions of the future. Therefore, since many of the prophecies have already come to pass, they can be tested in detail.

Good King Hezekiah ruled the southern kingdom of Judah from 715 to 687 B.C. The northern kingdom of Israel had been taken into captivity only a few years before he began to reign, and the victorious armies from Assyria menaced his borders continually. Midway in his twenty-nine-year reign Hezekiah fell dangerously ill, and having no heir at the time, he prayed that his life might be spared. God gave him a fifteen-year extension of life, announcing this good news through His prophet Isaiah. Isaiah also predicted that Hezekiah's descendants would be carried off to slavery in Babylon and would become eunuchs in the palace of the king of Babylon (Isaiah 39:5–7). This was a most unlikely prophecy at the time, since it was the King of Assyria who threatened Judah, and Babylon was only a vassal kingdom within his empire. Thoughtful persons who heard Isaiah make this prophecy might well have wondered whether he could be believed or not.

But almost exactly a hundred years later, Isaiah's remarkably detailed prophecy came true. During the century following the prophecy, Babylon threw off its Assyrian overlords and became once more master of the Mesopotamian region, and indeed the leading world power. Soon after this she conquered the kingdom of Judah, deporting the people to Babylon and making eunuchs of some of them in the palace of the king (Daniel 1:7).

The prophet Jeremiah lived to experience that captivity, and he predicted exactly how long it would last. In 605 B.C., when Nebuchadnezzar carried off the first group of Hebrews into captivity in Babylon, Jeremiah prophesied that the captivity would last exactly seventy years (Jeremiah 25:11). Who can see seventy years into the future? Economists today, with all their sophisticated charts and computer analyses, cannot even forecast the state of the economy six months in advance. Politicians are even wilder in their guesses! But Jeremiah said seventy years. And seventy years it was.

Not all believed him, of course. A false prophet named Hananiah challenged Jeremiah's forecast, declaring that Jeremiah was off by sixty-eight years! In just two years, said Hananiah, the king of Babylon will be defeated and the treasures of the Jewish temple which Nebuchadnezzar had looted would be returned to Jerusalem (Jeremiah 28:3, 4). Naturally, the people preferred to listen to Hananiah. Who wouldn't? But Jeremiah stood his ground, and in order to authenticate his long-range prediction about the seventy years of Babylonian slavery, he made a short-range one. He said that Hananiah would die within the year; unfortunately for Hananiah, Jeremiah was right (Jeremiah 28:16, 17).

Back to Isaiah

Isaiah carried on his long and active prophetic ministry from about 742 to 701 B.C., his death coming about one hundred years before Babylon took possession of Judah, and he predicted that it would happen. But even more amazing, he also prophesied what would happen to Babylon. He said that a group of people called the Medes would conquer and destroy Babylon (Isaiah 13:17–19). And so it was. On October 12, 539 B.C. Babylon was captured by Darius the Mede (Daniel 5:31), a feat that defied all logic, for the city of Babylon was an immense fortress. It was surrounded by an intricate system of double walls seventeen miles in length and wide enough for chariots to pass on the top. The walls were buttressed by defense towers and secured by massive gates, making the city virtually impregnable. But the conquerors were clever. They dammed up the Euphrates River which ran under those massive walls, and while the Babylonians were celebrating at a royal orgy, they marched under the walls upon the dry riverbed and captured the city.

Isaiah and Jeremiah passed the tests of a true prophet with flying colors!

The Ultimate Test

Since much of what you will read in this book explains the yet unfulfilled prophecies of the Bible, we ought to demand that the Bible pass a test vouching for the accuracy of its prophecies about events already consummated. Numerous prophecies in the Old Testament deal with the coming of Jesus Christ, and these provide an excellent test for the accuracy of Bible prophecies. If these were genuine prophecies (that is, written about events before they happened) and if they were fulfilled with detailed exactness, then we ought to sit up and take notice when the Bible predicts other events for the future.

Here is a list of some of the prophecies about the coming of Jesus Christ:

1. The prophet Micah predicted Jesus' birthplace 700 years before He was born. At the time it was a most illogical prediction, for Bethlehem was too small to have a place among the cities of Judah. Yet this insignificant village would be the birthplace of the Messiah.

2. The prophet Malachi, 400 years before Christ, predicted that Messiah would be announced by a "forerunner." John the Baptist fulfilled this prophecy (Malachi 3:1; Matthew 3:1–3).

3. Many details of Messiah's ministry were prophesied in the Old

Testament, details which were exactly fulfilled in the ministry of Jesus of Nazareth: its location (Isaiah 9:1, 2 and Matthew 4:13–16); its power (Isaiah 11:2 and Luke 3:22 and 4:1); its saving character (Isaiah 61:1 and Luke 4:16–19); its accompaniment by miracles (Isaiah 35:5, 6 and Matthew 11:4, 5); its inclusion of Gentiles and not merely Jews (Isaiah 42:1 and 6 and Luke 2:32); and the ultimate rejection by many (Isaiah 53:5 and John 1:11).

4. Heaped on top of these are additional prophecies about the death of Christ. It is one thing to predict the death of a world leader; it is something else to pinpoint with unerring accuracy the many details that the Old Testament relates about the death of Christ: where He would die, how He would die, by whom He would be killed, and the disposition of the body. Look at the following chart—and be amazed at the accuracy of Bible prophecy.

The Event Related to Jesus' Death	The Prophecy in the Old Testament	The Fulfillment in the New Testament
To be deserted	Zechariah 13:7	Matthew 26:31
To be scourged and spat on	Isaiah 50:6	Matthew 26:67
To be given vinegar to drink	Psalm 69:21	Matthew 27:34, 48
To be pierced with nails	Psalm 22:16	Luke 23:33
To be forsaken by God	Psalm 22:1	Matthew 27:46
To be surrounded by enemies	Isaiah 22:7, 8	Matthew 27:39, 40
To be numbered with transgressors	Isaiah 53:12	Mark 15:28
To agonize with thirst	Psalm 22:15	John 19:28
To commend His spirit to God	Psalm 31:5	Luke 23:46
To have His garments distributed	Psalm 22:18	John 19:23, 24
To have no bone broken	Psalm 34:20	John 19:33–36
To be buried with the rich	Isaiah 53:9	Matthew 27:57–60
To rise from the dead	Psalm 16:9, 10	Acts 2:27, 31
To ascend into glory	Psalm 68:18	Ephesians 4:8

From *The Bible and Tomorrow's News* by Charles C. Ryrie (Wheaton: Scripture Press), p. 59.

Jesus the Prophet

Jesus claimed to be a prophet; therefore He, too, must pass the tests for a true prophet of God. And He does. His predictions about His own death were definite and specific. He prophesied that someone close to Him would betray Him (Matthew 26:21), that He would die in Jerusalem, that His death would be instigated by the leaders of the Jewish people (Matthew 16:21), that He would die by crucifixion, and that three days later He would come back to life (Matthew 20:19).

So when you read the next chapter about Jesus' predictions of the future, remember that He has passed the tests of a true prophet. He deserves a hearing. He came, He ministered, He died, and He rose from the dead exactly as He and the Old Testament prophets predicted.

Only Two Options

I have cited only about thirty predictions concerning the ministry of Jesus Christ, but there are many more: upwards of three hundred, to be exact. Now, there are only two options as to how such a large variety and number of prophecies could be accurately fulfilled: either the prophets who predicted these events—and the Bible that recorded them—are true and accurate, or it all happened by chance.

Let's put that "chance" option to the test.

Let's Flip Over It

If you take a coin, say a dime, and flip it twice, there are four possible results: it will land heads both times, or tails both times, or heads then tails, or tails then heads. So the chance of its landing heads both times is one out of four. Or, to put it another way, if four people each flipped a dime two times, one of them could be expected by the laws of chance to come up with two heads in a row.

The chance of getting heads three times out of three flips is, of course, greatly reduced. If eight people each flipped a dime three times, one of them could be expected to come up with three heads. One person in sixteen could expect four heads in an uninterrupted sequence, and so on.

If slightly more than a thousand people were all flipping dimes a thousand times, chances are that one of them would turn up heads ten times in a row without any tails breaking the sequence.

To get twenty heads in an unbroken sequence would require more than a million people; an uninterrupted run of thirty heads, more than a billion people.

A run of forty heads in forty flips could happen by chance less than once in a trillion times. Or, if there were 4 billion people on each of 250 earths like ours, and if all of them were flipping dimes, then chances are only one of them could be expected to come up with forty heads in forty tosses.

Now, think of each prophecy about the life of Christ as a coin flip, and each accurate prophecy as a flip that comes up heads. If every person living when Christ was born were to have made thirty predictions concerning His life, the odds are that not one of them would have scored 100 percent on his guesses. Every living person would have been stoned as a false prophet!

But there are more than thirty predictions about Jesus.

Suppose you wanted 100 heads out of 100 tosses. The probability of doing this is less than one in 1,000,000,000,000,000,000,000,000,000,-000,000! But such a number is incomprehensible, so we need a comparison to help us understand it.

Astronomers tell us that there are something like 200 billion stars in the Milky Way. Imagine that on each of these 200 billion stars live 4 billion people. The population of all the stars of the Milky Way would add up to a figure with only twenty zeros. Now, if all these people were flipping dimes, not one of them would come up with twenty heads in twenty flips. Or if all of them were trying to predict twenty things about the coming of Christ, every person would be stoned as a false prophet. Not one of them would be able to do it accurately by chance. (From *The Bible and Tomorrow's News,* pp. 61–63.)

Chance No Choice

Therefore, if it wasn't chance or luck that guided the prophets of the Bible, what was it? The only other option is that God did it. No wonder the Bible, in which these prophecies are recorded, is such an unusual book.

But not all the prophecies of the Bible have come to pass. Many remain to be fulfilled. And if history teaches us anything, it teaches that we can count on their being fulfilled in every detail.

What of the future? In the following chapters you will find Jesus' forecasts of coming events. You'll discover how the nations of the world will eventually line up. Will Russia and China pose a united threat to the West? Will the West ever be a great power bloc again? What role will the Arab nations play? Will Israel survive? What about the United States? Will communism take over the world? What role will the Church have in world affairs? Will peace ever come?

The Bible has true answers for you to all these questions. Keep a copy handy and read them for yourself as we proceed.

2

The Worst Is Yet to Come

Worldwide famine.

Recession.

Doomsday.

Armageddon.

Security eludes us. The foundations of society seem to be crumbling beneath us. Long-range planning is impossible. No one seems to know what lies ahead.

But Jesus knew. And He has presented His credentials and passed the tests of a true prophet. It would be wise for us to listen to His forecasts.

His Swan Song

The occasion was Jesus' farewell message to His puzzled band of disciples. After more than three years with Him, they still did not fully understand what was shortly to happen to their Leader. Three days later, on that fateful Friday, He would lie in a tomb: silent, cold, dead, cruelly tortured and crucified by Roman soldiers. But for now it was Tuesday of that last week of His life, and from the vantage point of the Hill of Olives, Jesus was about to unveil a panorama of the future to His disciples.

Twelve men, each immersed in his own thoughts, slowly climbed to the summit of the hill. After the Master had seated Himself on a rock, Peter, James, John, and Andrew approached Him to ask the question that had been burning in their minds for many days (Mark 13:4). Finally, the boldest member of the group inquired, "Rabbi, when will the world come to an end?" The little band sat facing the setting sun, Jerusalem spread out in silhouette two hundred feet below them. They watched as thousands of pilgrims flooded into the city in anticipation of the Passover celebration. Soon the twenty-four gates of the temple would be closed for the night. As the shadows length-ened over the Holy City, the greatest prophet Israel had ever known began to paint a dark and gloomy picture of the future. Yes, the worst was yet to come.

The Temple Will Topple

Herod's temple was a magnificent structure. Dominating the entire city, it occupied the northwest corner of a plateau roughly one thousand feet square, on an area that had been artificially leveled at immense labor and cost. The main temple structure, begun in 20 B.C., was completed ten years later, but the process of building on the temple site continued until A.D. 64, a generation after the death of Jesus. The entire plateau was flanked by a continuous wall constructed with porticoes and supported by gleaming white pillars. Ten thousand workmen, employed to cut the massive stones required for the project, were joined by a thousand priests specially trained in masonry and carpentry, whose job it was to work on the most sacred parts of the building. The immense foundation stones, made of white marble overlaid with gold, measured as much as thirty-seven by twelve by eighteen feet, and many ten to twelve feet in length were plainly visible.

Imagine the disciples' consternation, therefore, when Jesus announced that not one of these great stones would be left upon another, but that each would be thrown down (Matthew 24:2). It couldn't be, they reasoned. The temple was still in the process of being built. How could He dare to speak of its destruction?

Titus Did It

But scarcely was the temple and its complex of buildings completed when Christ's words came true. The long-smoldering discontent between Jews and Romans finally erupted in A.D. 66. The legate of Syria drew first blood by attacking Jerusalem, then quickly withdrew. Nero immediately sent his ablest general, Vespasian, to quell the revolt. Beginning in the north, Vespasian attempted to subjugate the country before making a direct attack on the capital. By a quirk of political fate his plans were changed, for in A.D. 69 he was made emperor. Returning to Rome, he left the conquest of Jerusalem to his son Titus.

Titus went about the task with deadly precision. A siege was begun which was to last for 134 days. Jerusalem, already packed with refugees fleeing the advancing Roman army, was further laden with pilgrims who had come to celebrate the Passover. Famine wracked the city. The number of dead quickly mounted. With the city under siege, there was nothing left to do but stack the bodies like firewood in the streets. Estimates placed the number of dead between 200,000 and 600,000. In the end, the temple and the city were reduced to ashes. Though Titus attempted to preserve the magnificent temple by ordering it left untouched, the Roman soldiers were not to be denied. Seizing the opportunity to vent their hatred for the stubborn, always resistant Jews, they reduced the temple to a heap of rubble. Ultimately, only the three great towers of Herod's palace were left standing, and that in order to protect the camp of the Tenth Legion, which remained behind to guard the site.

The remainder of the city was dug up to its very foundations. Using long bars, the Roman soldiers pried apart the massive stones of the temple in order to reach the gold and silver which had been stored there for safekeeping. When they had finished, not one stone remained upon another. Jesus' incredible prediction had come true. Yet, despite the terrible carnage and senseless destruction of Jerusalem, the worst was yet to come.

Passing the Test

It is important for a prophet to establish his credentials by predicting events which in fact do come to pass before too long, and while the prophet is still alive and active. Anyone can predict events hundreds of years down the corridors of time, with the smug assurance that he will have long since passed from the scene before history can prove him wrong. Thus it was essential, as a practical consideration, for prophets in ancient times to give a prediction of something that would happen in the near future. If and when it indeed came to pass, others would know that he was a true prophet and worthy to be trusted in his long-range, less easily verifiable predictions. This is precisely what Jesus did that evening on the Hill of Olives. He boldly predicted the destruction of Jerusalem and the temple, and roughly forty years later His prophecy was fulfilled to the letter.

History tells us that He passed the test. Since He has been proved correct so many times in the past, why should we not assume that the remainder of His predictions will also occur just as He said?

Telescoping the Future

The Roman conquest of Jerusalem was only a preview of what will take place in a future day. In fact, most of Jesus' final message to the disciples spoke of that future time. Jesus used the prediction of events in 70 A.D. as a kind of prophetic springboard to more distant happenings. He was telescoping prophecies, a device which is not unusual in the Bible. The prophets Daniel, Isaiah, and Zechariah all wrote predictions which intermingled near and far events, so it is not surprising to find that Jesus did it also.

Three of the Gospel writers give us accounts of Jesus' final message. The shortest is found in Luke (21:5–38). Mark's record of the discourse occupies chapter 13 of his Gospel. Matthew's account is by far the most detailed (chapters 24, 25), and so we'll study the panorama from his perspective.

The Disciples' Questions

Three questions were on the minds of the disciples that evening as they sat together with their Lord on the brow of the Hill of Olives. "When shall these things be?" they asked incredulously, in response to His assertion that the massive stones of the temple would be overthrown. Luke's record gives us the answer: "When Jerusalem is surrounded by armies," as it was in that fateful year 70. "What shall be the sign of Your coming, and what shall be the sign of the end of the age?" they asked further. To the Jewish mind of that day, the end of the age was commonly associated with the intervention of God into human history by means of the personal return of the Messiah. Today two thousand years have come and gone since those questions were first asked, making the need for clear answers even more relevant. What will be the signs of the end of the age? How can I know when the second coming of Jesus Christ will climax history? Are there any signs on the horizon today that point to the end of the age being very near?

Hard Times Ahead

One thing is crystal clear in Jesus' answer: This world is not going to get any easier to live in. Almost unbelievably hard times lie ahead. Indeed, Jesus said that these coming days will be uniquely terrible. Nothing in all the previous history of the world can compare with what lies in store for mankind. "For then there will be great distress, unequaled from the beginning of the world . . . and never to be equaled again" (Matthew 24:21 NIV).

But hasn't the world seen difficult times before in history? Aren't millions of people suffering extreme hardships right now? Why will these coming days be so vastly worse?

Two reasons. First, the distress and despair will be on a worldwide scale. One religious magazine stated that the second most significant religious news story of 1974 was "worldwide persecution." The editors noted that increasing numbers of Christians were being caught in a massive spread of the use of torture and other police-state control at the hands of those in power in countries in the Far East, Africa, and South America. Add to this the continuing repression of Christianity in the Soviet Union and in China, and persecution appears to be fast assuming worldwide dimensions.

Second, the coming days will be unique because as the end approaches, people will realize that time is running out. They will do more than just talk about the "hard times." They will begin to act as if they truly believe that the end is near. Words like "Armageddon" and "holocaust" have crept into our newspapers and magazines with increasing frequency in recent years. But when the end comes, people will stop talking and start acting. And their actions will take the form of self-destruction, as they seek to take their own life before the world ends it for them.

Pseudosaviors

There will be no lack of religion at the end. A great ecumenical church will arise (more about this in chapter 11). Many religious leaders will cry for attention, offering "salvation" from human needs. "Many shall come in my name saying, 'I am the Christ.' But," the Lord continued, "they shall deceive many" (Matthew 24:3). These false saviors will realize that there is nothing to be gained by a direct frontal attack on God and religion. Rather, their plan will be to encourage a subtle, almost imperceptible break with religion by substituting good things for the best things. "After all," they will argue, "what could be better than a solution to the world's problems?" Ever increasing numbers of these pseudosaviors will offer solutions for symptoms, rather than a cure for the disease. They will seek to avoid the root problem, the problem of sin and estrangement from God— the problem which a true Savior must deal with.

The same Jesus who predicted a steadily blackening picture for the world is the Jesus who would state hours later, "I am the way—and the truth and the life. No one comes to the Father except through me" (John 14:6 NIV). Earlier in His ministry He had promised, ". . . whoever comes to me I will never drive away" (John 6:37 NIV). Obviously, He was setting Himself in stark contrast to these fakers, claiming to be the one and only true Savior. Who cannot recall reading about at least one of the many self-styled saviors: fanatics offering the millennium, gurus claiming to be divine. Many have captivated large audiences and collected millions of dollars from the unsuspecting public. But ultimately they are phoney. They sell pep, not purity; help, not holiness; temporary lifts, not eternal life. *Beware, said Jesus, for they shall deceive many.*

How are these people going to be fooled, to be duped into accepting solutions that treat only symptoms and fail to give real inner peace? In Matthew 24:23–25 we learn the answer. These false, self-proclaimed saviors will accredit themselves with "great signs and wonders." They will back up their claims with miracles. And it is by means of these miraculous signs that many will be deceived, for they will reason this way: Any religious teacher who can perform supernatural feats must have something worthwhile to say. What sort of miracle will these men perform? One great religious leader who is prophesied to appear during that terrible time of future trouble will have the power to give life to an inanimate idol (Revelation 13:15)!

We are almost deceived when Walt Disney creates an image of Abraham Lincoln which can rise from a chair, recite famous passages from Lincoln's addresses, gesture to the audience, and sit down again.

Imagine what would happen if that fake Lincoln actually came to life. Not just get up from a chair, but actually walk right off the stage at Disneyland, mingle in the crowds, and make some predictions about the future of the stock market. Suppose Mr. Disney (if he were living) should appear and say, "I did it. I made him alive." Jesus warned: "If it were possible, they shall deceive the very elect." And it is easy to see why.

But beware, for this very thing is happening now. Not the giving of life to an idol, but the appearance of some remarkable and inexplicable signs and wonders. Persuasive prophets and teachers aided by printed and audiovisual media are captivating millions. Standing in opposition to all such, and standing patiently outside our all-too-closed doors, is Jesus Christ. Years ago Jesus accredited Himself by means of the greatest miracle ever performed, a miracle unequaled before or since. Three days after His crucifixion, He rose from the dead, not merely in spirit but with a new body as well. And this resurrected Savior has stated, "No one comes to the Father except through me." He can be trusted.

War, War Everywhere

Here is another scene from Jesus' panorama of the end. Wars. Rumors of wars. Continuous conflict between nations (Matthew 24:6). Two great world-engulfing wars in this century; civil wars in China and South America; bitter, persistent fighting in Southeast Asia and the Middle East. Men talk peace and fight wars, and Jesus predicted that this would continue right up to the end. There will be no lasting peace on earth until the Prince of Peace comes again.

Upheavals

Famines and earthquakes (Matthew 24:7). How suddenly the worldwide food shortage of 1974 overtook the world, catching even the experts by surprise and plunging the world into a food crisis. The U.S. Department of Agriculture predicted bumper crops during the summer of 1974. They did not bargain with the weather, and the rains came too little and too late. In Pakistan the situation was destructively reversed. Too much rain washed away the food that was so desperately needed. The price of fertilizer skyrocketed on the world market, depriving the very nations who needed it most and could afford it least. Famine led to starvation, and starvation to death. The cycle was predictable, yet unavoidable.

Earthquakes pose a different problem. They can be studied and recorded, but not prevented. They kill and destroy with frightful suddenness and ferocity. In recent years earthquakes have ravaged cities from California to Turkey, and yet they do not compare with some that will yet occur. A terrifying quake will shake the world at the beginning of that unique time of trouble which is yet to come, causing people to seek death rather than trying to go on living (Revelation 6:12–17). Another will destroy one-tenth of the city of Jerusalem, leaving seven thousand dead in its wake (Revelation 11:13). But the worst earthquake ever to befall mankind will take place at the very end of that unique period. As though it had already happened, so clear is John's vision, Revelation describes it as "unlike any other, so tremendous was the quake" (Revelation 16:18).

There is no place to hide during a severe earthquake. The ground shakes violently and rolls in undulating waves. Fissures appear without warning in what was previously unbroken terrain. Buildings topple, showering debris upon any who are unfortunate enough to be standing nearby. Natural and man-made shelters are practically useless. It is a terrifying experience.

Hatred and Persecution

Godliness has never been one of the more popular virtues. The Egyptians despised the Hebrews. So did the Canaanites. Jesus Christ was hated and rejected. Thus it was natural for Jesus to warn His followers that the world would hate them because it first hated Him (John 15:18).

More Christians have died for their faith in the twentieth century than in any other, including the first. It is claimed by some that upward of 15 million Christians have been slaughtered in Russia and other Communist-controlled countries. Why do people hate the followers of Christ with such a vengeance? Jesus answered that question long ago: "Everyone who does evil hates the light, and will not come into the light for fear that his deeds will be exposed" (John 3:20 NIV).

The situation will deteriorate, rather than improve, for future disciples of Christ. In the quiet beauty of that evening setting, Jesus painted a bleak picture for the followers of Christ, a picture even darker than the one we have seen in the past history of the Church. "Then you will be handed over to be persecuted and put to death," He predicted, "and you will be hated by all nations because of me. At that time many will turn away from the faith and will betray and hate each another. . ." (Matthew 24:9, 10 NIV). He envisioned torture, death, hatred, and desertion. Even some of those professing to belong to God will find the going too rough and will desert, leaving the true followers of Christ to stand alone.

Antichrist

But the worst is yet to come. Introducing His disciples to the most sinister figure ever to invade human history, Jesus described Antichrist's determined campaign to obliterate God's people in a future day.

No single descriptive term can completely sum up the vile character of Antichrist. His name betrays his basic stance—he is unalterably opposed to Jesus Christ and all that He stands for. Christ is God; Antichrist is man. Christ is God personified; Antichrist is humanity in all its bankrupt glory. Because of his ferocity Antichrist is pictured as a beast (Revelation 11:7; 13:1). He is designated a king who "will do as he pleases and. . . will exalt and magnify himself above every god. . ." (Daniel 11:36 NAS). Paul called him "the man of lawlessness" and "the man doomed to destruction" (2 Thessalonians 2:3 NIV). Not a pretty picture.

Antichrist's actions are in step with his character. Jesus introduced him to the disciples that evening as "the abomination that causes desolation" (Matthew 24:15 NIV), an echo of something the prophet Daniel had prophesied six hundred years before (Daniel 8:23–26; 9:27; 11:36). Daniel warned the world that this man would come; so did Christ; so did the apostles Paul and John. Yet in spite of these numerous cautions concerning Antichrist, when he finally appears he will be hailed as a savior, a man to bring order out of political and economic chaos, a man who deserves to be worshiped.

More of his political career later. Right now let's follow him as he commences his program of persecution against God's people during those unique days of trouble ahead.

The Signal

"When he stands in the Holy Place," warned the Lord, "then watch out!" To the Jewish mind that could only mean one location: the temple. But as we have seen, Titus reduced the Jews' beloved temple to a heap of rubble in A.D. 70. Could it be that the long-cherished dream of the Jewish people to rebuild their temple in Jerusalem once again will someday be fulfilled? Jesus predicted such an event. So did the apostle Paul, who said that the Antichrist would "sit in the temple of God, showing himself as God" (2 Thessalonians 2:4). The temple of A.D. 30, whose awesome size and grandeur amazed the disciples, would soon be destroyed. But another would be built in the future, Jesus promised. But for nearly two thousand years the Jewish people have had no temple, their sacrificial worship system is no more; instead, they worship in synagogues. Some day that will all be changed, and the Holy City will once again boast a temple with its sacred Holy Place.

The people's joy will be short-lived, however. For though they will be able to worship in their temple for a time, they will not be free to worship their God. The monotheism of Judaism will suddenly be replaced by the godless Antichrist, who will sit in the Holy Place demanding to be worshiped. Every true follower of Christ will be repulsed by such a brash display of blasphemy and pride.

Worship or Die!

In order to enforce his self-worship, Antichrist will launch a campaign of intense persecution aimed at those who refuse to comply. The persecution will center in and radiate from Jerusalem. Jesus warned against remaining in the area once Antichrist's program of annihilation begins. "If you are in Judea get out quick. Don't go back home to pack clothes. When the signal flashes [that is, when Antichrist enthrones himself in the temple], then flee to the mountains" (Matthew 24:16–18).

The timing of such a flight will be all-important. "Pray," Jesus continued, "that your flight doesn't have to be in the winter or on the Sabbath." Winter weather could greatly hamper the efforts of Jesus' followers to get out of the city quickly, especially if it were on the occasion of one of Jerusalem's rare snowstorms.

If Antichrist chooses to begin his reign of terror on the Jewish Sabbath (i.e., Saturday), the situation will become immensely more complicated. Public transportation will be scarce. People will be unprepared for an evacuation. The Yom Kippur War in 1973 showed the extent of disruption caused by an enemy attack on the Sabbath. The outbreak of hostilities on that particular holiday nearly cost Israel her national life. Perhaps Antichrist will launch his religious attack on a Sabbath and thereby gain an initial advantage in his campaign to usurp God.

Armageddon

The climax is coming, and it is Armageddon. Jesus told His disciples three things about it on that quiet evening long ago.

First, it will involve a carnage of unbelievable proportions. "Wherever there is a carcass, there the vultures will gather" (Matthew 24:28 NIV). And there will be carcasses aplenty. In his vision of that final battle, the apostle John saw an angel calling to all the birds of the heavens to come to Armageddon and devour the bodies of the slain, "the flesh of kings, and the flesh of captains, and the flesh of mighty men, and the flesh of horses, and of them that sit on them, and the flesh of all men, both free and bond, both small and great" (Revelation 19:18 KJV).

Second, the heavens will be shattered by a series of terrifying catastrophes. The sun will quit shining. The moon will be blacked out. Stars in the sky will fade from view. It is noteworthy that Isaiah predicted these same events some seven hundred years before Christ did: "The stars of heaven and the constellations thereof shall not give their light: the sun shall be darkened . . . and the moon shall not cause her light to shine" (Isaiah 13:10 KJV).

Third, Christ will make His long-awaited reappearance, when men shall see Him "coming in the clouds of heaven with power and great glory" (Matthew 24:30 KJV). Many will welcome Him gladly; others will not. But with the second coming of Christ will come the welcome assurance that the worst is over, and the best is yet to come. Christ's return will mark the end of those terrible days of suffering and persecution. But the darkness must come before the dawn.

Putting It All Together

In one of the greatest single prophecies recorded in the Bible, Jesus told His disciples that the worst was yet to come. He described the upheaval of the stones in Herod's temple, a seemingly impossible feat which the Roman soldiers accomplished in A.D. 70. By correctly predicting the fall of Jerusalem and the destruction of the temple, Jesus authenticated His credentials as a prophet, giving us confidence in the reliability of those predictions which are yet to be fulfilled.

The years ahead will be characterized by false prophets, wars, upheavals in nature, and persecution. The time will draw to a close in a climactic period of the most intense trouble the world has ever experienced. This period of distress will last for seven years, as we learn from other Bible prophecies, and will be dominated by the archenemy of Christ. Antichrist will set himself up as God and demand universal worship. Using political, military, and economic forces, he will attempt to bring the entire world under his control, even challenging Christ Himself at the very end. Global warfare will climax in the campaign of Armageddon, at which time Christ will return to put down all opposition, bring justice to the earth, and reign as victor. The worst will be over, and the best years the world has ever seen will be inaugurated by Jesus the Messiah.

3

Europe Will Rise Again

Italy on Verge of Bankruptcy!
British Pound Slips Again on Multibillion Trade Deficit!
Inflation Rampant in European Countries!

So read the headlines of the 1970s. Once-mighty Europe seems to be on a decline from which there is little prospect of recovery. But Europe will rise again, united and powerful in world affairs.

Almost everyone knows about Daniel in the lions' den. But Daniel also sat in the prophet's chair. Jesus validated his credentials by calling Daniel a prophet (Matthew 24:15).

And two of the greatest prophecies about Europe's future come from Daniel.

Nations Come and Go

Every nation assumes it will exist forever. Assyria thought it would, and with good reason. That great empire dominated the biblical world most of the time from the ninth to the seventh century B.C. But the Assyrian rule was replaced with startling suddenness in about sixty years' time. Nebuchadnezzar, a great general and second king in the restored dynasty of the Babylonian royal house, called by historians the Neo-Babylonian Empire, dealt a series of stunning deathblows to Assyria. In addition, he won an outstanding victory over Necho of Egypt at Carchemish in 605 B.C., and conquered and destroyed Jerusalem in 587 B.C. At this strategic point in world history, Daniel and others were carried to Babylon as slaves of Nebuchadnezzar.

"Uneasy lies the head that wears a crown," especially during the lonely night hours. When Nebuchadnezzar went to bed he worried about the future. True, he was sitting on top of the world, but what about five or ten years down the road? What did the future hold for him and his kingdom? Conquest? Revolution? Assassination?

"As for you, O king, while on your bed your thoughts turned to what would take place in the future; and He who reveals mysteries has made known to you what will take place" (Daniel 2:29 NAS).

God visited Nebuchadnezzar in a dream (Daniel 2:1). Dreams are fine if you can be sure of what they mean. But Nebuchadnezzar couldn't. So he did the only thing he knew to do. He called his wise men together and demanded they tell him not only the interpretation but also the contents of the dream. Now, no ruler had ever put wise men to such a test before. Usually the king told them the dream and they told him the interpretation. Of course, that way the wise men could make up any interpretation that came to mind. But by having to tell the king the dream, as Nebuchadnezzar was demanding, they were on the spot to prove that they really could see into the unknown. In effect Nebuchadnezzar was saying, "If you can read my mind, I'll be sure you can read the future." But naturally they couldn't, for they were not true prophets.

Would the Real Prophet Please Stand Up?

So Daniel asked the king for a little time (Daniel 2:16), and asked God for a lot of wisdom. Then he appeared before the king and told him the dream and its meaning. I can just see Nebuchadnezzar nodding his head as Daniel rehearsed the dream. "Yes, that's right. That's exactly what I dreamed. Go on, Daniel." And we can be sure the king was all ears when Daniel began to interpret the meaning of the king's dream.

A Statue Speaks

The king saw a magnificent statue, resembling a man, which depicted the next four great world empires. Nebuchadnezzar was the part of the statue represented by the head of gold. The breast and arms were identified as the kingdom that would succeed Babylon, the Medo-Persian empire. The belly and sides represented Greece, the successor to Persia. The legs and feet were Greece's successor, Rome.

"Impossible," Nebuchadnezzar must have thought. "No one will ever displace me. How could anyone ever conquer this great city that I have built?" (Daniel 4:30). He had reason to wonder. Babylon's walls were 87 feet thick and 350 feet high. More than a million people lived within its fourteen-square-mile area. To the Greeks its famous hanging gardens were one of the seven wonders of the ancient world. Its fortifications seemed impregnable.

But Babylon did fall. Four kings and twenty-one years after Nebuchadnezzar's death it came to a sudden end when on October 12,

539 B.C. Darius the Mede conquered the city (Daniel 5:20). Babylon, the kingdom built to endure forever, lasted exactly eighty-six years.

The Persian empire fared a little better, lasting 208 years before Alexander the Great put an end to it in 331 B.C. The successors to Alexander's empire in the east—the Seleucids of Syria and the Ptolomys of Egypt—one or the other, held sway over Palestine for 268 years more before Rome took over.

Focus on Rome

"Legs of iron, feet of iron and clay." The metals in the statue decrease in value but increase in strength from top to bottom. Gold is soft, but iron is hard. One historian said of Rome, "To resist was fatal, and to flee was impossible."

But what about those toes? Part iron and part pottery indicates that some form of the Roman empire will lack unity and strength. Ten political elements will exist simultaneously, thereby diluting the strength of the kingdom.

Daniel the Dreamer

Daniel also had a vision, and it covered the same sweep of history, the same four world empires. This vision is recorded in Daniel 7. He saw four beasts, and the fourth, representing the Roman empire, was different from all the others (Daniel 7:23). Great iron teeth devoured and crushed its foes (Daniel 7:7), an apt figure for the manner in which Rome operated. The western Mediterranean, which became a Roman lake in the second century B.C., was only the beginning of Roman conquests. Palestine fell to Rome in 63 B.C., and soon all of the territory eastward to the Euphrates was under Roman control. What is today Great Britain, France, Belgium, Switzerland, and most of Germany was also conquered. Daniel's predictions came true.

Ten Horns and a Little Horn

"It had ten horns. . . . Another horn, a little one, came up among them, and three of the first horns were pulled out by the roots before it; and behold, this horn possessed eyes like the eyes of a man, and a mouth uttering great boasts" (*see* Daniel 7:7, 8 NAS). Ten toes on the statue. Ten horns on the fierce animal. Ten kings represented by the ten toes and ten horns. An angel interpreted the meaning for Daniel (verses 24 and 25): This is Rome revived.

Better Luck Next Time

Not that there haven't been other attempts to bring the pieces of Rome together since its disintegration. Charlemagne tried in A.D. 800, but his empire was nothing compared to the glory that was Rome. Napoleon tried and failed. Hitler likewise. But the man depicted as the "little horn" will attempt it once again, and he will prove successful.

When?

Back to the statue for a moment. There was a fifth kingdom in Nebuchadnezzar's dream, represented by a stone which destroyed the statue and then grew until it filled the whole earth. When will the eternal kingdom of God come? "In the days of those kings [represented by the ten toes] the God of heaven will set up a kingdom which will never be destroyed . . . it will crush and put an end to all these kingdoms, but it will itself endure forever" (Daniel 2:44 NAS). Here's an important clue! The ten-nation form of the revived Roman Empire will exist just prior to the return of Christ to set up His kingdom on earth.

In the last chapter we surveyed Jesus' picture of the unique time of great trouble that is coming. Part of that scenario will be the formation of this ten-nation federation in the geographical area once ruled by Rome. Located west of Palestine, it might best be labeled the Western Federation of Nations, or the United States of Europe. But whatever the name, the form is clear: ten nations banded together to form a mighty power bloc during those years just prior to the return of Christ.

Little But Potent

A little horn, Daniel called him (Daniel 7:8), but he was a mighty voice. He is the leader of the ten-nation federation. He is the Antichrist whom Jesus told His disciples about that evening on the Mount of Olives. He is the abomination that makes desolate (Matthew 24:15). Jesus talked about Antichrist's religious activities, whereby he will enforce the worship of himself. Daniel foresaw his political activities as head of this alliance of nations.

What will cause ten proud, independent nations to unite like this under a single ruler? The Bible does not say, but we do know there will be other great power blocs during those years, indicating that self-defense may be one reason. Economics may dictate such a union.

The concentration of wealth in Arab nations in the east could easily force the western nations to unite politically in order to survive. Military threats from Russia and her satellites may also be involved. In any case, current events are rapidly leading to this final union.

NATO and the Common Market

NATO has seen better days, but one serious threat from a powerful nation such as Russia could rejuvenate NATO overnight. At present the emphasis of the Common Market is largely economic, but even today there are political overtones. In the future it may gain or lose world importance, but the organizational structure is there, and overnight it could easily be turned into the political base of operation for Antichrist and his allies. Today there are nine nations in the Common Market. Tomorrow there may be eleven or eight, but one day there will be ten, no more and no less.

Recent developments point to the increasing importance of the Common Market to global economics. In rapid-fire succession, the following took place within the span of a single week in May 1975: Mexico opened talks to explore the possibilities of economic ties with the Common Market; China agreed to send an ambassador to the European Economic Community, thus becoming the first Communist nation to recognize the Common Market countries as a bloc; and Israel concluded a far-reaching trade pact with the Common Market despite an Arab League warning of possible political consequences.

Internal Struggles

The revival of Europe will not come without struggle. Antichrist himself may take the lead in forming the union, or the nations may come to the place in their unification efforts where they will be searching for a leader. Economic and/or political circumstances may force the sudden emergence of that leader. In any case, his rise to power will be quick and startling. Since he comes from among the ten kings, according to Daniel's vision, he must come from one of the countries which will form the union. He must come from a country in the same geographical area as the old Roman Empire. Since the federation will exist as a power bloc in the years immediately preceding the coming of Christ, it is safe to make this prognosis: If the coming of Christ occurs in the next thirty to fifty years, this man is alive somewhere on earth today. He will be a strong leader, for ten nations will not give up their sovereignty easily. He will prod them into joining the federation. His name and accomplishments will be headline material during those first years of unprecedented trouble.

But force will be necessary, too. Daniel saw the little horn subduing three of the ten kings (Daniel 7:20). Obviously not all the nations will be happy about losing their independence, even though pressure to do so will be heavy, and three will resist. Whether Antichrist will have to use military force or will be able to accomplish the unification by other means, we do not know, but three of the ten nations will join the federation grudgingly and under compulsion.

Antichrist will boast of great things. No doubt he will promise solutions to the major problems of the day. During the Israeli-Arab Six-Day War, one high U.S. official publicly stated that if only someone would tell him what to do, he would do it. The world situation when Antichrist comes to political power will be plagued with severe problems. Remember that Jesus predicted famines, earthquakes, and wars. Leaders will grope in vain for solutions to the crises, eventually crying out that if someone, anyone, would tell them what to do, they would do it. And Antichrist will gladly issue the orders.

Power at a Price

Europe will rise again, but at terrible price. Antichrist will be a political savior, but a spiritual devil. Europe will regain tremendous power, but at the cost of losing all spiritual and moral values. Antichrist will wage war against the saints and overpower them (Daniel 7:21). He will speak out against the true God (Daniel 7:25). He will intend to change times and laws. He will exercise almost absolute power. But not quite. For God will still be in control, and Antichrist's zenith of power will last only three and one-half years. For seven terrible years he will dominate the world scene, and during the last half of that time he will appear seemingly invincible. But God will never lose control, never give Antichrist more power than he should have, and never be caught by surprise by the newspaper headlines.

Putting It All Together

The Common Market and the fortunes of Europe may have their ups and downs, but over the long haul (which won't be any too long!) the fortunes of Europe are moving toward a climax of power. Despite whatever delays may interrupt the development in Europe, look for signs of increasing unity. When that unique seven-year period of trouble begins, ten nations will emerge and form a federation. Three of them will balk at such a union. A strong leader, Antichrist, will emerge who will force the three reluctant ones into the merger and, along with the other seven, forge a ten-nation power bloc.

What geographical area will be encompassed by this federation? The simplest answer is the area covered by the old Roman Empire, but at various stages in history this has meant different things. However, a map of the Empire before its division in A.D. 395 shows Rome ruling all of southern Europe, England, North Africa, Greece, and areas in western Asia, including Palestine.

Enter Palestine

But Israel will not be one of the ten nations in the federation. She will be aligned with the ten-nation federation by means of a treaty. One of the first accomplishments of Antichrist as head of the federation will be to take Israel under his political wing. He will successfully negotiate a treaty with the Jewish people which will guarantee them certain rights: political security and certain religious freedoms. After the Six-Day War in 1967 the world thought Israel was invincible. The Yom Kippur War in October 1973 changed that idealistic notion, and demonstrated that Israel was only human after all. She may win or lose again before signing the treaty with Antichrist, but sign the treaty she must. She will not be able to go it alone but will need the support and protection which an alliance with that great power in the west can give her.

Under the religious aspects of the treaty, Israel will be guaranteed the right to establish worship once again in a temple at Jerusalem. A dream nearly two thousand years old will finally come true, and it will be the Antichrist who will make it happen.

But religious freedom won't last for long. The tenuous peace will continue a meager three and one-half years. Then all hell will literally break loose. The treaty will be shattered. Antichrist, with his political power fully consolidated, will set out to conquer the world. He will be opposed by other alliances of nations, but world domination will be his goal, and he will stop at nothing less. Given enough time he might succeed; but time will run out, and Christ will come. Armageddon will be Antichrist's Waterloo. Christ will be his Wellington.

"And I saw Antichrist, and the kings of the earth, and their armies, assembled to make war with Christ and with His army. And Antichrist was taken . . . and cast alive into a lake of fire burning with brimstone" (Revelation 19:19, 20). What an inglorious end to a spectacular career.

What to Look For

In view of such remarkable prophecies, look for these events and trends:

1. Increased ease of communication. These coming events will occur rapidly, necessitating rapid means of communication, including satellite TV.

2. External pressures placed on Europe, forcing European nations to unite.

3. A European quest for a leader to solve pressing problems. Several may arise and fall, but someday one will emerge to dominate the scene.

4. Increasing economic controls. One of Antichrist's weapons will be economic. He will not permit people to buy or sell without his stamp of approval (Revelation 13:16, 17). A checkless society, where all monetary transactions are handled by computers, would facilitate this.

5. European self-sufficiency. This does not necessarily mean she must produce internally all the natural resources and manufactured goods she needs, but such resources must be made available and secure for her. Recent oil discoveries in the North Sea could easily make her independent of Middle East oil in the near future.

Europe may be down momentarily, but she is not out. Europe will rise again, to become the most influential power bloc in the world just before the end.

4

You'll Need Blue Cross

Seven years is a long time. Seven years represents 84 months, or 364 weeks, or 2,556 days, or 61,334 hours, or 3,680,640 minutes, or 220,838,400 seconds. That's a long time. And to rephrase an old bromide, time passes very slowly when you're not having fun.

Jesus, you'll remember, labeled those seven years as a period of distress unique in the history of the world. No other era begins to match that one for pure human misery. To be sure, time will seem to move at a crawl during those seven years.

Revelation Is a Revelation

Many people are fully convinced that the last book in the Bible is impossible to understand. As a result they ignore it completely. How strange! For that last book is named the Revelation, a title which is taken from the first verse of the book. Now a revelation is just that: a revelation, not something hidden. The dictionary defines a revelation as "an enlightening or astonishing disclosure." A revelation reveals, divulges, discovers, discloses. And that is precisely what the Book of Revelation is: an enlightening and astonishing disclosure. Take heart, for Revelation can be understood.

The natural response is: *How?* How do we make sense out of all those beasts and thrones and horsemen and huge numbers like 200 million? Answer: Take it at face value. If God intended to disclose something to us in a book, then we can be confident He wrote it in such a way as to communicate to us, rather than confuse us.

But someone is quick to raise the cry, "What if I cannot understand everything He has said to me in that book?" No one in his right mind would pretend to understand everything in the Bible, but that shouldn't push us to the other extreme where we give up trying to understand anything! Much of the Bible is crystal clear, sometimes painfully clear, and those are the parts we need to give primary attention. When tackling any new or unfamiliar book or passage in Scripture, I've found it's a good procedure to begin with the portions

I understand. Then I use that information to help clarify the portions I don't understand. Usually this technique works, with the result that what I do understand increases, and what I do not understand diminishes. Plenty of facts concerning the coming seven-year period of trouble are quite clear in the Revelation. These are the facts which we can, and must, understand.

A Free Jailbird

The apostle John wrote the Revelation. He came from a fairly well-to-do family in Galilee, where along with his father Zebedee and his brother James he lived the rugged outdoor life of a fisherman. He must have been a man of action, not the effeminate person often portrayed by artists, for he was known as a "son of thunder." With his brother James and his fellow fisherman Peter, he formed the inner circle of Jesus' disciples.

In later life he became the recognized leader of all the churches in Asia Minor (western Turkey), and he himself apparently lived at Ephesus. Reliable stories not found in the Bible tell of his vigorous activity and staunch defense of the faith to the end of his long life. Some would say he was too aggressive for his own good, for he was later jailed for his efforts, not in an ordinary jail guarded by bars, but one surrounded by water. Sometime in the 90s he was arrested by the Roman Emperor Domitian and banished to the small island of Patmos in the Aegean Sea southwest of Ephesus, where he worked in the mines.

Why did the old man John find himself in such wretched circumstances? "Because of the Word of God and the testimony of Jesus" (Revelation 1:9 NIV). John had thundered his witness for the faith once too often. The emperor thought to silence him once and for all by exiling him to a lonely and desolate island. But silence and thunder fare poorly together. John used the opportunity instead to write the last great book of the Bible. Ironically, from his isolated dungeon John penned a message which was to spread throughout the world. Messengers, the emperor learned, can be bound; God's message cannot.

Unroll the Scroll

There were no paperback books in ancient times. Books were made in the form of scrolls. Pieces of leather or papyrus about ten inches wide were pasted together to form a continuous roll. After a scribe had finished writing a section of the scroll he would stop, roll up the scroll to that point, and seal it. Then he would begin again, stop, roll up the scroll, and affix another seal. In this way he prevented any unauthorized person from tampering with or divulging the contents of the scroll. Only a duly authorized person could break those seals.

Sometimes a man's last will and testament was secured with seven seals. When a Jewish family was forced to sell its property or possessions, the loss was listed on a scroll and sealed seven times. By law, the property could not be taken away from them permanently, so the scroll contained the record of the loss and what would have to be done in order to get the property back. When a qualified person came along to redeem that property, then it was returned to the original owners.

It was just such a scroll, rolled up and sealed, that John saw in his dream (Revelation 5:1). What did it mean? Apparently it recorded man's right to rule upon earth. When God created Adam He gave him dominion over the earth (Genesis 1:26). Then one day a snake appeared, who was the devil, the great usurper, and he too wanted to rule the earth. In order to do that, he had to corrupt man first. You know the story from there. Adam and Eve were enticed to rebel against God, from whom they had derived their authority to rule. They disobeyed by eating the forbidden fruit, were expelled from the garden, and lost their right to rule the earth.

And who do you suppose took over the reins of rulership? Satan. For these thousands of years since the fall of man, Satan has been promoting his plan and program upon earth. What exactly is that plan? Though many-faceted, Satan's plan is to separate men from God and to perpetrate the deception that man is the captain of his soul, the master of his own fate, and has no need of a savior other than himself. Now and then the devil permits man to experience some success in controlling his environment or making his life better. But in the long run man has consistently come out the loser. His life expectancy has dwindled to barely one-tenth of what early man enjoyed. His environment sickens by the day. Man-made religions fail to meet the need for inner peace and contentment. World peace remains only a glimmering mirage on the distant horizon. Obviously man has lost his God-given rights. The devil seems to have things well in hand. The scroll is tightly sealed.

Unseat the Usurper

Is there anyone who can break the seals and redeem the situation? If there is, he must be stronger than the devil. And there is. John described Him as "a Lamb having been slain" (Revelation 5:6). He stepped from the throne of heaven, took the scroll, and began to unroll it in order to unseat the usurper once and for all.

But it will not be an easy process. There is a revolution that must be crushed. Many knowingly or unknowingly have enlisted in the devil's army. The devil himself must be cast out, and all who follow his plan must be punished. All this is painful but necessary if man is to regain his original privileges.

Revelation chapters 6 through 19 describe the process in graphic detail. It may be hard to imagine a God of love acting in such fierce wrath and judgment—but remember, for thousands of years He has been trying to coax man back to His side, offering him the free gift of salvation through Jesus Christ His Son.

Relatively few have accepted the offer. Most have merely given God an ungrateful slap in the face, and then continued on in their rebellious ways. In that coming time of unique trouble, however, God's patience will finally come to an end. Forced to resort to sterner measures, God will crush all rebellion and return the rule of this world to Jesus Christ and His followers.

On and On and On

Seven years will seem like an eternity when the punishments and judgments begin to fall. The seals on the scroll will be broken open. Every time one is opened, a terrible catastrophe will occur. But when the seventh seal is broken, instead of the end of judgment there will be a crescendo as seven trumpets suddenly appear. As each one of these is blown another judgment falls. When the seventh trumpet is sounded and the end appears in view, the intensity of judgment will crescendo again as seven little bowls appear. Each time one is emptied, another punishment will appear. Only after the seventh bowl has been emptied will the end come, as Jesus Christ Himself returns to this earth to rule in righteousness and to restore peace and justice to all creation.

Seven seals, with the seventh revealing seven trumpets; seven trumpets, with the seventh announcing seven bowls of wrath. Then, and only then, will the final curtain drop.

Let's sketch what will happen in each of these judgments, and show why men will need Blue Cross (though Blue Cross will probably go bankrupt long before the end).

Cold War (Seal No. 1 : Revelation 6:1, 2)

Cold war is a term invented after the end of "hot" World War II, to fit the postwar period of tension—but the Bible described it nineteen hundred years ago. John predicted the arrival of a leader who will conquer without breaking the peace, and that's a perfect description of cold war. Who will this conqueror be? We have already met him in Jesus' farewell message to His disciples. He is Antichrist, the abomination that causes desolation. When that unique seven-year period begins, Antichrist will begin to enlarge his territory by cold war tactics. Many will consider him a savior; in reality he will be the devil's greatest ploy.

The apostle Paul predicted that at the beginning of this final act of human history, the world will be saying, "Peace . . . safety" (1 Thessalonians 5:3). Judging from the signs of the times and the seeming nearness of the end, there may never be a World War III. We may experience relative peace with only small fires to put out here and there in the world, but no worldwide conflagration. Or it is equally possible that a world war could break out, in which case a time of peace will follow before Antichrist begins to implement his final takeover. In either case the peace will be an uneasy one. The masses will eagerly believe Antichrist when he promises to bring about a just and lasting peace. But that hope will quickly be shattered.

Hot War (Seal No. 2 : Revelation 6:3, 4)

Peace will vanish like an early morning dew under the midday sun, and open war will burst upon the world. Perhaps at this time the Russian bear will arise to pounce upon Palestine (as described in chapter 5). War will capture the headlines, and will continue unabated until Christ returns. No peace is possible without the Prince of Peace.

Famine (Seal No. 3 : Revelation 6:5, 6)

Suddenly John saw a black horse and a rider with a pair of scales in his hand, carefully rationing the basic foods needed for human survival. Jesus predicted famine. John described the severity of it: "A quart of wheat for a denarius, and three quarts of barley for a denarius . . ." (NAS). A denarius was the average day's wage for a rural worker in Bible days. Today, John's statement would sound something like this: "$30 or $40 for a quart of wheat." If you think supermarket prices are astronomical today, imagine paying $40 for a five-pound bag of flour! With that little bit of flour you must feed your entire family, and there is no assurance when you will be able to buy more, even if you have the money.

Looking at it another way, normally a denarius paid for eight quarts of wheat or twenty-four quarts of barley. Thus, the basic food supply will be slashed to one-eighth of normal. There can be only one result: worldwide famine of unprecedented magnitude.

Death (Seal No. 4 : Revelation 6:7, 8)

Only one of the famous Four Horsemen of the Apocalypse is named, and he is Death. Death claims the body, for only the body dies. The soul of every man exists eternally. That is why Death is accompanied by Hades, for Hades claims the souls of those who reject the true Savior. Death and Hades are the Grim Reapers, and John sees them reaping a bountiful harvest. One-fourth of the entire population of the earth will be destroyed at this time, killed by a combination of war, famine, plagues, and disease. The plagues may be the natural consequences of war and famine, caused by man's inability to dispose of the ever increasing number of decaying bodies. Or perhaps the plagues raise the awful specter of bacteriological warfare. Almost overnight man's dreams of peace, plenty, and longevity will vanish.

Murders (Seal No. 5 : Revelation 6:9–11)

Jesus warned of martyrdom; John filled in the details. To follow Christ will mean constant surveillance by Antichrist and, for many, death at the hands of his agents. But for these martyrs, as for all followers of Christ, "to die is gain," for they will spend eternity with Him in heaven. What a stark contrast! To follow Christ will mean physical death, but eternal life. To follow Antichrist will mean physical life, but eternal death.

Terror (Seal No. 6 : Revelation 6:12–17)

Six catastrophic events will strike terror in the hearts of men. A great earthquake will jar some part of the world, perhaps caused by a nuclear explosion, perhaps decimating populated areas and killing millions. The sun will be blackened and cease giving its light. The moon will turn blood red. The earth will be pummeled by a meteorite shower of unequaled magnitude.

To date, the largest meteorite ever to strike the earth weighed

132,000 pounds. One meteor slammed into Arizona, leaving a hole 4,150 feet wide and 570 feet deep. In 1908 the famous Tunguska meteorite crashed to earth in Siberia. People hundreds of miles away saw it in full daylight, and the resulting blast was felt fifty miles away. By comparison, this future meteorite shower will be like standing under a tree of overripe figs, and having all the fruit fall at once. Only these will not be figs, but meteorites weighing tons apiece.

Perhaps the greatest terror of this judgment will occur when people look for a safe place to hide, and find none. Every mountain and island will be jarred from its present position. People will seek to hide in caves and among the rocks of the mountains. In utter desperation they will even pray to the rocks to fall on them and kill them, but death will elude them. People will realize that these catastrophes are from God, that it is He who is pouring out wrath and judgment upon the earth. Yet they will not turn to Him in repentance and faith. Instead, they will seek to hide from His presence in much the same way that Adam and Eve avoided a confrontation with God long ago in the Garden of Eden.

This is only the beginning. The worst is yet to come.

Vegetation Destroyed (Trumpet No. 1 : Revelation 8:7)
When the seventh seal is broken, seven more judgments will occur, announced to John by the blowing of seven trumpets. The first will destroy one-third of the trees, grass, and grain-producing vegetation. Without plant life the topsoil will quickly erode away, resulting in floods and climatic disruptions. One catastrophe will snowball into another.

Oceans Bloodied (Trumpet No. 2 : Revelation 8:8, 9)
Something will fall into the oceans of the world: perhaps an H-bomb, perhaps something that hasn't yet been invented. Whatever the cause, the results are clear. One-third of the sea will turn to blood, and one-third of all sea life will be killed. One-third of all the ships will be destroyed. In an instant, all the great naval powers of the world will have their flotillas cut by one-third. All fleets of merchant ships will be depleted by one-third. The number of oil tankers will suddenly be reduced by one-third. Food supplies will fluctuate wildly as one-third of all fish are instantly killed, and the rest are polluted. Movement of supplies will grind nearly to a halt because of the scarcity of ships. Havoc will come to industrialized nations, for neither raw

materials nor finished products will be able to move freely in and out of the countries of the world. Once again, the snowballing effects will be more severe than the judgment itself.

Water Pollution (Trumpet No. 3 : Revelation 8:10, 11)

Fresh water will become a thing of the past. Forced to drink water that is bitter to the taste and polluting to the system, many people will die from the contamination. Pollution will exist on a scale the world has never known.

Recycling the Cycle (Trumpet No. 4 : Revelation 8:12, 13)

A recent ad in the newspaper pictured a bright sun rising on the horizon, with the caption: "Just as you can count on the sun rising tomorrow morning, you can count on your money being safe in our bank." But one day the twenty-four-hour cycle of day and night will be recycled. The sun, moon, and stars will be darkened, changing the normal cycle by one-third. No one is quite sure whether this means we will have sixteen-hour days or twice as much darkness as in a normal twenty-four-cycle. In either case, the productivity of the earth's crops will be sharply curtailed.

Woe to the World

The worst is still yet to come! The remaining three trumpets are so much worse than what has preceded them, that they are called "woes." It is not difficult to understand why.

Locusts from the Pit (Trumpet No. 5 and Woe No. 1 : Revelation 9:1–12)

This judgment comes right out of hell. Literally. Up to this point men will battle over men, and the destructive forces of nature will be unleashed; but now hell gets into the act. The abyss is unlocked, smoke billows forth, and out of the smoke come locusts. But this is no ordinary brand of locust. John found himself groping for words as he attempted to describe them. They are like horses, and they sound like a thundering army. They will sting people like scorpions for a period of five months, yet their sting will not be fatal. People will be tormented to the point of crying out for death, but death will not come. J. A. Seiss has described their agony this way: "The pain from the sting of a scorpion, though not generally fatal, is perhaps the intensest that any animal can inflict upon the human body. The insect itself is the most irascible and malignant that lives, and its poison is like itself" (*The Apocalypse,* II, 83). But remember that these "locusts" are from hell. They will be demons that take grotesque shapes and torment men with their sting. They will be organized and under the command of a very powerful demon who is appropriately named the Destroyer. They will be "locusts" gone wild.

If demons seem out of place in our twentieth century society, don't be fooled. Jesus battled demons. The apostle Paul faced their attacks. Today's generation is much more "with it" than previous generations when it comes to recognizing the power of Satan. And someday the whole world will be exposed to this horde of demon-locusts.

John's description sounds very much like some kind of war machine or UFO. Demons have the ability to take different shapes, so it is quite possible that John is picturing a coming invasion of warlike UFOs. Until someone comes up with a satisfactory answer to the UFO question, this possibility should not be ruled out.

Manipulated Media

How will the news media explain these colossal headlines of a future day? Undoubtedly, reasonable attempts will be made to explain the famines and diseases. But how will world leaders explain away the changes in climate and the day-night cycle? What will they do with the locust-demons? Manipulated news and censored reports will help, but when people can look out their windows and see for themselves, the commentators will be hard pressed for answers. Huge amounts of money will probably pour into disaster areas. There will be speeches and crash programs in the United Nations. But these will serve only as salve to deceive the world's leaders into thinking they are still masters of their own fate.

Overpopulation Solved (Trumpet No. 6 and Woe No. 2 : Revelation 9:13–21)

Woe to the world, for another army is about to be loosed. It will number 200 million (Revelation 9:16), will flow from the east (more about that in chapter 7), and will kill one-third of those still living on the earth. When the fourth seal was opened, one-fourth of the population was destroyed. Now a third of the remaining ones will be killed. In these two catastrophes alone, the world population will be cut in half. In fact, because of disease, famine, war, martyrdom, there will be fewer than 50 percent of the world's inhabitants left to experience the remaining judgments.

Imagine the long obituary columns in the papers, the constant stream of funeral processions, and the pallor of death that will hang over the world like smog. Surely the people will return to God now! But no, instead of worshiping God they will worship "demons, and idols of gold, silver, bronze, stone and wood" (Revelation 9:20 NIV). Why? Because idols that cannot see or hear or talk cannot make demands upon men. Men can control an idol; it cannot control them. And so men will live as they please and worship dead inanimate idols, even in the face of terrifying destruction all around them.

Seven More to Come (Trumpet No. 7 and Woe No. 3 : Revelation 11:15–19)

When the seventh trumpet blows the end will be in sight, but not before seven final judgments fall. These are described in Revelation 16 as judgments poured out of bowls.

Mass Malignancy (Bowl No. 1 : Revelation 16:2)

Antichrist will not be able to help his followers now. God will send painful sores on all those who follow Antichrist, and he will be powerless to cure them. Possibly the phrase used to describe these sores means malignant, indicating some sort of cancer. During World War II, survivors of Hiroshima and Nagasaki developed disfiguring sores because of their exposure to the radiation. Perhaps the same will be true here.

Bloody Seas (Bowl No. 2 : Revelation 16:3)

Seventy-two percent of the surface of the earth is covered by oceans. As a result of the second-bowl judgment, all that water will turn to blood, killing every creature in the seas. The stench and disease brought about by such a calamity will be indescribable.

Bloody Rivers and Lakes (Bowl No. 3 : Revelation 16:4–7)

The supplies of fresh water will also be turned to blood, and there is a reason. Because men will kill God's followers during this time, they will be forced to drink blood in grim retribution.

A Heat Wave (Bowl No. 4 : Revelation 16:8, 9)

The strength of the sun will be heightened so that it will scorch men with intense heat. And nothing but bloody water to drink!

Darkness (Bowl No. 5 : Revelation 16:10, 11)

While most of the world is sweltering in blistering heat and brilliant sunlight, just the opposite will be true in Antichrist's capital. There will be pitch darkness. Activity will grind to a halt, perhaps preparing the way for the armies of the East to sneak across the Euphrates River.

No Pontoon Bridges Needed (Bowl No. 6 : Revelation 16:12)

As Antichrist prepares to capture the world, a great army from the East marches to stop him (more of this in chapter 7). The great Euphrates River marks a natural boundary and must be crossed. There is no way around. Imagine being an engineer in the front lines of that army, preparing to build a pontoon bridge, when suddenly the river dries up right before your eyes. You radio your commander at the rear of the column to tell him that the river has just disappeared. No need for pontoon bridges now! No need for delay in marching right into Palestine. Shouts of praise ascend to heathen gods. March on, you armies of the East. God has dried up the Euphrates, not your puny gods. March on, for you have an appointment with Him, to fight with Him face to face at Armageddon.

The End of the World (Bowl No. 7 : Revelation 16:17–21)

If you were to plan a movie of the end of the world, the script would sound something like this: "There came flashes of lightning, rumblings, peals of thunder and a severe earthquake. No earthquake like it has ever occurred since man has been on earth. . . . The cities of the nations collapsed. . . . Huge hailstones of about a hundred pounds each fell upon men. And they cursed God on account of the plague of hail, because the plague was so terrible" (Revelation 16: 18–21). That is exactly how John describes it. Only this isn't the end of the world, just the end of what used to be the world. The seventh bowl marks the end of the period of great distress just before Jesus Christ returns to bring in a new world. Think of it. All the great cities of the world leveled. Tokyo, Mexico City, London, Rome, your hometown. Every man-made monument reduced to rubble before human eyes. Think of it. An earthquake of a magnitude unique in all the world's history. Hailstones weighing a hundred pounds each. Think of it. Men hurling blasphemies at the true God, while serving dumb idols of wood and stone and metal. Think of it.

Unbelievable? Perhaps. But inevitable nonetheless. Jesus sketched the broad outline of those seven terrible years for His disciples that quiet evening. John filled in the frightening details.

Why will God allow these awful things to happen to men? Rebellion must be punished. The devil's kingdom must be crushed. Jesus and His followers must exercise their prerogative of dominion over the earth. For thousands of years God has tried in vain to convince men to follow Him. In the face of continuing rebellion, God has no alternative but judgment. And yet, even in judgment, God is restrained and gracious. At first, only one-fourth of the population is judged, but men do not repent. Then a third is burned or polluted, but men do not repent. Finally the judgment is universal, but—incredibly—men still do not repent. Even in judgment, God is always there patiently waiting, waiting, hoping that men will turn again to Him.

5

The Bear Will Hammer Away

What will Russia do?

Few diplomatic or military moves have been made in the past thirty years without leaders' first asking that question. In the past twenty years Russia's interest in the Middle East has risen dramatically. At times she has been deeply involved. At other times she seems to withdraw. One thing is certain: Russia plays the diplomatic game with self-interest uppermost in every action she takes.

In 1974 *U.S. News & World Report* (April 29) concluded: "Whatever strategy the Russians adopt . . . one thing seems evident: They do not intend to abandon their efforts to hold and expand the position they carved out in the Mideast over the past twenty years."

What will she do? Will the United States and Russia confront each other in a nuclear war? Will communism take over? Will Russia have allies in the Middle East? Again, the prophecies of the Bible have the answers.

Ezekiel, Front and Center

Twenty-five hundred years ago the prophet Ezekiel predicted an invasion of Israel by a great power. At this point reading Ezekiel 38 and 39 will be illuminating. Ezekiel saw a mighty army coming against the land of Palestine (Ezekiel 38:15, 18). Some strange-sounding names are given to the allies that make up this attacking force, but where it comes from is clear: the remote parts of the north. Remembering that prophetic directions are always in relation to Palestine, this means that the attack is launched from some country north of Israel.

Is Russia Named?

Gog, Magog (chief prince of Meshech and Tubal), Persia, Cush, Put, Gomer, Togarmah. Few would recognize any of these names, with the exception of Persia, though some were mentioned in lists of countries in Genesis 10 and in 1 Chronicles 1:5, 6. But these are the peoples and lands Ezekiel saw involved in this great invasion of Israel. Who are they?

Gog and God

Scholars aren't sure of the exact derivation of the word *Gog.* Some think it comes from a word that means "darkness." That certainly fits within the character of Gog as described by the prophet Ezekiel in chapters 38 and 39 of his prophecy. Others think it comes from a root word that means "to be high." And that too fits his character as a proud, important ruler. He's related to the land of Magog, wherever that is. Possibly he is the ruler of Magog. And that fits, because Gog is used as a title, much like King, or President. Indeed, in the Greek translation of the Old Testament (made about 250 B.C. for Greek-speaking Jews in Alexandria and called the Septuagint), Gog is used as a title for kings. In one interesting place in the Septuagint it is used to translate the name of Agag (Numbers 24:7), and Agag was an archenemy of God's people, the Jews.

Putting that all together, what do we come up with? Just this: Gog is the ruler or leader of the people who live in Magog, and he is against God all the way.

Where Is Magog?

Josephus, the great Jewish historian of the first century, in his work called *Antiquities* identified Magog as those "who are by the Greeks called Scythians." But where is Scythia? The dictionary identifies it as "the country of the ancient Scythians comprising parts of Europe and Asia now in the U.S.S.R. in the regions north and northeast of the Black Sea and east of the Aral Sea." A glance at a map shows clearly that this means territory now occupied by Russia. Couple this identification of Magog with Ezekiel's statement that the invaders of Palestine would come from the "remote parts of the north" (38:15 NAS), and all the vast territory of the land of Russia looms large and menacing in Ezekiel's prophetic picture. The land of Magog, then, is the land of Russia.

Russia today is the largest country in the world, covering more than half of Europe and nearly two-fifths of Asia. It is almost as large as all of North America, and occupies more than one-seventh of the world's total land area. With a population of approximately 260 million, it has the largest armed forces of any country in the world:

an estimated 3 million men in uniform. And some day all these men and materials will be mobilized against the land of Israel.

The Allies

Ally No. 1 is "the chief prince of Meshech and Tubal." Attempts have been made to relate these to the modern Russian city of Moscow and the Russian province of Tobolsk, but there is no support for this. Rather, these names probably refer to peoples who lived east of Greece in what is modern-day Turkey.

You will notice if you compare English translations of Ezekiel 38:2 that some read differently and say "the prince of Rosh, Meshech and Tubal." *Rosh* is a word which means "chief," so the translation "chief prince" is correct. But others believe Rosh is an early form for the word Russia, reinforcing the identification of this enemy of Israel as that great northern power. To sum up: Ally No. 1 is Turkey.

Ally No. 2 is Persia (verse 5). The modern name for this country is Iran. It lies south of Russia and east of Turkey. And it is rich in oil!

Ally No. 3 is Ethiopia, or Cush. This is not modern Ethiopia but northern Sudan, lying just south of Egypt. A fascinating feature of the culture of this land in Bible times was its close ties with India and Persia by means of the sea route around southern Arabia. This is the area from which the Ethiopian eunuch mentioned in Acts 8:26–30 came. Though far removed from Russia, Cush may well be linked with the alliance in a coming day because of a prior link with Persia, or Iran. Certainly such an ally would protect the southern flank of the Russian invaders.

Ally No. 4 is Libya, or Put. This is the area west of the Nile delta which is occupied today by Libya. And who hasn't heard of Libya and her strong anti-Israeli stand? She will make a logical ally for any enemy of Israel in a coming day. And she is rich in oil!

Ally No. 5 is Gomer (verse 6). The identification is debated, but it appears to refer to the area of Cappadocia, which is in the eastern part of Turkey, and possibly the Ukraine, which is in European Russia north of the Black Sea.

Ally No. 6 is Togarmah, which is in the southeastern part of Turkey near the Syrian border.

Look at a map and you will see the intriguing gap in this alliance. Russia is, of course, the chief power. To the south she is joined by

Turkey and Iran. Then add the two isolated allies, Sudan and Libya. The gap is obvious—it is the Arab states that ring Israel. Lebanon, Syria, Iraq, Jordan, Saudi Arabia, and Egypt are all missing from this Russian alliance. And no wonder, for they will form a bloc of their own to continue to harass Israel until the end.

Feeling Left Out

It's practically impossible to imagine Russia left out of anything going on in this world. But apparently that's the way it's going to be.

Since 1954 Russia has made every effort to make her influence felt in the strategic Middle East. And she has been successful. Her heaviest economic investments have been in Egypt, Syria, and Iraq. She has invested in the Aswan Dam in Egypt, the Helouan Steel Complex in Egypt, and the Euphrates Dam in Iraq. In 1954, for example, Egypt imported 1.5 percent of her total imports from Russia; in 1970 that figure rose dramatically to 47 percent. Educated guesses as to the total economic aid Russia supplied during the period from 1954 to 1970 place the amount at $2 billion to Egypt, $750 million to Syria, and $3 billion to all the other Arab countries combined.

Even greater in dollar terms have been Russia's persistent efforts to gain military leadership in the Arab lands. Through 1970, arms and equipment totaling nearly $6.7 billion had been supplied by Russia to Arab countries. Of this total, Egypt received about $4.5 billion.

But all this to no avail. Russian arms and influence reached a zenith in the Yom Kippur War of 1973. Since then her influence has diminished. It is the United States that has taken the lead in peace efforts. Russian attempts to send additional military experts have been rebuffed. Egypt has been shopping in the French jet supermarket. The oil embargo of 1973–74 totally reversed the foreign policies of many nations, causing them suddenly to find new friends among the Arab countries.

Oiling the Machinery

The oil-exporting nations with their sudden enormous wealth are looking to the industrial nations of the world for purchases and investments. They are not recycling their billions of petrodollars through Russian banks, and they are not buying rubles with their dollars and pounds. The oil-producing nations are entering into trade agreements with the oil-consuming nations. It just makes good economic sense.

Russia, of course, is not dependent on the Arab nations for oil. Actually, known reserves of oil in Russia are greater than those in the United States. The oil-producing nations realize they need to spend their great wealth in those countries which buy their oil, and Russia is not one of them. Furthermore, they know that the oil-consuming nations need a ready market for the materials they produce. We've seen dramatic proof in recent years that foreign policy can be easily modified and even turned around by economic pressures. So the Arab nations are no longer dependent on Russian arms. They can buy Western technology, and Western foreign policy won't stand in their way.

Out in the Cold

This kind of picture leaves Russia out in the cold. She cannot twist Arab arms by offering Russian arms. Further, the Arab nations do not need economic aid now. But Russia needs the land bridge and sea gateway to other parts of the world that Palestine offers. What can Russia do? Her presence throughout the world depends in some measure on her naval power. And naval power depends on freedom to move through the Suez Canal, the Red Sea, and the Indian Ocean. Such freedom of movement will be an absolute necessity when Antichrist forms his alliance in the West, effectively blocking the Mediterranean for his own use. If Russia cannot go west, she must look east, and that means she needs to dominate Palestine.

Headlines in the *New York Times* on March 2, 1975 confirmed this: "Soviet Said to Expand Air and Naval Activities in Persian Gulf Area" and, "Opening of Suez Benefits Soviet Missions in Persian Gulf and Indian Ocean."

So what will she do? If military and economic aid will not be needed by Middle East countries, she will have to resort to military intervention if she intends to control that important bridge of land and water. When the time is right, she will launch the attack described so long ago by Ezekiel.

The Horses Are Coming

A cavalry in this day of jets and atom bombs? It does seem unbelievable. But Ezekiel saw the mighty army from the north coming against the land of Israel on horses (Ezekiel 38:4, 15). Of course, this means an overland attack down through Turkey, which, you will recall, is Ally No. 1 of Russia during the invasion.

But on horses? Possibly Ezekiel used that term simply because he knew no word for tanks or planes. But it is equally possible he used the word because the army will in fact use horses. While there have been no horse cavalry units in the United States Army since 1943, it is true that horses were used in World War II. In fact, the Russians reportedly used 300,000 horse cavalrymen during that war.

Can any of us predict what conditions will be like when this future invasion occurs? We do know that commerce and industry will be greatly disrupted during that seven-year time of trouble. In fact, the disruption may be so complete as to make mechanized equipment scarce. And if tanks and planes are scarce, what will they use? Horses?

A glance at the map shows something else as well. Any attack by land through Turkey will have to cross several mountain ranges (three to be exact). The Caucasus Mountains, the Pontic Mountains, and the Taurus Mountains all lie between Russia and Israel via Turkey. When Persia, Ally No. 2, joins the attack, her armies will also have to cross the Elburz Mountains and the Zagros Mountains before entering Israel. And when they arrive in Israel there will be more mountains (Ezekiel 38:8; 39:17). If the troops cannot be airlifted across those mountain ranges, they will have to cross them somehow by land: perhaps in mechanized vehicles, perhaps on horseback, perhaps both, reserving the cavalry for more effective warfare on the mountainous terrain of much of the land of Israel itself.

What's in It for Russia?

Why all this effort on the part of a country that is already immense? We have already noticed the strategic geographical location of Israel. But there's more to it than that. Russia will make an all-out effort to capture slaves, to take booty, to plunder, to carry away gold and silver (Ezekiel 38:12, 13). Why will Russia need these things? She probably won t, and yet she will still invade. Why? Listen to Ezekiel again: "You will devise an evil plan" (38:10 NAS). Sheer hatred for Israel will be one motivation for the attack. Hatred of the Jews, the strategic location of the area, and the wealth of the land will spur Russia on to the conquest.

Who Will Bury Whom?

When Nikita Khrushchev honored the United Nations by pounding his shoe on the table, he declared that Russia would bury the

United States. He obviously had not read his Bible recently. God said that Israel would bury Gog with all his multitude (Ezekiel 39:11). And where? In a valley east of the Dead Sea (39:11). Ironic, isn't it? Gog and his armies will go to Israel to capture and plunder the land, intending to use that valley as a highway to world supremacy. Instead, that valley will become their graveyard. So jammed will it be with corpses that no one will be able to traverse it.

Who will defeat such a vast army? God Himself. Ezekiel says that God will send an earthquake and fire to destroy them. Israel will not even have to defend herself, at least not against this army, for God will win the victory for Israel.

The Vultures Will Be Busy

The cleanup job will be colossal, for this will be no ordinary victory in battle. If it were, then the victims could be buried gradually over a period of time, as they were killed. But when such a large number of soldiers die all at once, in a moment of divine intervention, then the job of disposing of the bodies and weapons will be one of gigantic proportions. How will this be accomplished?

Bonfires. Bonfires of weapons. No fuel shortage for Israel then. In fact, not for seven years. That's how long it will take to dispose of the weapons, and all during those years "they will not take wood from the field or gather firewood from the forests, for they will make fires with the weapons" (Ezekiel 39:10).

Grave-digging. Seven months will be required to bury the dead. But that won't be enough time to complete the job, so God will step in and speed things up. He will summon the vultures of the skies and the animals of the earth to expedite the removal of the corpses:

> And you will be glutted at My table with horses and chari-
> oteers, with mighty men and all the men of war. . . .
>
> Ezekiel 39:20 NAS

When, Pray Tell?

No specific answer to this question is given to us by Ezekiel, but he does drop some clues.

Clue No. 1: The invasion will come when the Jewish people are back in their land (38:8). Since Titus captured Jerusalem in A.D. 70, the Jewish people have been scattered throughout the world. There was little thought of returning to Palestine until early in the present century. Then suddenly Zionism blossomed, and with the blessing of the United Nations the Jewish State of Israel was born in 1948, and since then the Jewish people have been returning in unprecedented numbers. In the first twenty-five years of the existence of the State of Israel the population has increased fivefold! Ezekiel's prophecy could not have been fulfilled fifty years ago. But today it can, and soon it will.

Clue No. 2: When the invasion comes, Israelis will be living securely, in unwalled cities (38:8, 11). Israel will feel safe and secure. That is not true today, nor will it be true until Israel has negotiated that treaty with Antichrist which will guarantee her borders and the safety of her way of life. So the Russians will have to come sometime during that seven-year period of trouble. Probably they will come during the first half, just before Antichrist turns traitor to Israel. During that time Antichrist will consolidate his own political gains in the west. He will formulate his Grand Plan for world conquest. Israel will depend on him for her security, and lulled into a false security, she will be open to sudden attack from the northern army.

A Peek Into the Looking Glass

What does all this say about what we may expect to see happen in the near future?

It says that Turkey will move out of the orbit of Western influence and cooperation, and move into the sphere of Russian domination. What will trigger this, we do not know. But eventually Turkey will align herself with Russia and her other allies.

It says the same for Iran, since Persia will also be a Russian ally in the coming war.

It says that Russia will never dominate the entire world. Israel will be her enemy. The Arab nations, except for Libya, will not be aligned with Russia. The Western bloc under Antichrist will be against Russia. The nations of the Far East will be a power bloc separate and distinct from Russia, so we may confidently say that Russian influence will never become worldwide. Russia may export her communism, but communism will never serve as the adhesive force to bring nations together politically.

One final word: After the darkness of this awful period will come

the brilliance of Israel's greatest day. More of that later, but hear
Ezekiel once more:

> Now I shall restore the fortunes of Jacob, and have mercy
> upon the whole house of Israel; and I shall be jealous for My
> holy name. And they shall forget their disgrace and all their
> treachery which they perpetrated against Me, when they live
> securely on their own land with no one to make them afraid.
>
> Ezekiel 39:25, 26 NAS

The worst and the best are still ahead for Israel. Only bad times
lie ahead for Russia.

6

News From the Nile

Herodotus, the great Greek historian, called Egypt the gift of the Nile. And so it is, for the floodwaters of that great river deposit rich, black soil on the land year after year, sustaining the very life of the nation. Beyond the river stretches the barren wasteland of the Sahara, the largest desert in the world. So it is not surprising that 99 percent of the Egyptian people today live along the Nile or near the Suez Canal.

More than five thousand years ago Egypt rose to a place of prominence in the world. Tourists today come from all parts of the world to see the mighty monuments and temples of ancient Egypt. The magnificent pyramids enshrine the tombs of the mighty pharaohs. The Great Sphinx, a 240-foot-long statue carved from solid rock and stone blocks, stands like a sentinel over the land, vividly reminding us of the greatness of ancient Egypt.

The Egyptians developed the world's first national government. Their religion emphasized a life after death. They created an expressive art and literature. They introduced stone architecture. They produced the first convenient writing material, papyrus. They developed a 365-day calendar. They made pioneer breakthroughs in the fields of geometry and surgery.

Fertile Black Gold

Ancient Egyptians called their country Kemet, which means black, referring to the land. The fertile black soil deposited by the Nile drew Abraham to Egypt in order to escape the famine in the land of Palestine (Genesis 12:10). About two hundred years later Joseph was sold into slavery in Egypt by his jealous brothers. Soon, famine in Palestine forced his entire family, seventy members in all, to migrate to Egypt. From these seventy grew the mighty nation of Israel, numbering several million by the time of the exodus from Egypt under Moses four hundred years later.

Solomon also enjoyed the fruits of the fertile black land. He married Pharaoh's daughter and enjoyed lucrative commercial relations with Egypt, including a monopoly on the horse and chariot trade, because he controlled the land trade routes between Syria and Egypt (1 Kings 10:28, 29).

Israel's Enemy

Historically, enmity has characterized Egypt's relations with Israel. Solomon was an exception. Solomon's successor, King Rehoboam, felt the iron hand of Egypt when Shishak, king of Egypt, conquered Jerusalem in the fifth year of Rehoboam's reign and looted all the treasures of the land (1 Kings 14:25, 26). Pharaoh Necho conquered Palestine during the reign of King Josiah. The great prophet Jeremiah died in Egypt after he had been taken there a captive.

Only Egypt's eclipse as a world power cooled her continuous conflict with Israel. The Assyrians, the Babylonians, the Persians, the Greeks, the Romans, the Arabs, the Turks, Napoleon, and finally the British all took their turns conquering Egypt. Beginning with the pharaohs, Egypt lived under various forms of royal rule for five thousand years, until she became a republic in 1953 under Mohammed Naguib and Gamal Abdel Nasser.

Then the old enmity erupted again. Egypt, along with the other Arab League nations, went to war with Israel when the Jewish state was established in 1948. The years that followed saw almost continuous border skirmishes and snipings with Israel. During 1955 Israeli and Egyptian troops clashed along the Gaza Strip of northeastern Egypt, while Egypt seized the Suez Canal from its British and French owners. The following year British, French, and Israeli troops tried to recapture the canal, bombing Egyptian military bases and capturing Port Said. The United Nations arranged a truce, and a peacekeeping force policed the area until Egypt demanded its withdrawal just prior to the Six-Day War in June 1967. The results of that war are well known: Egypt was pushed back to the canal, suffering territorial losses in the Sinai which were only partially regained in the Yom Kippur War of 1973. At this moment, sensitive negotiations continue in an effort to ease the tensions between these archenemies, but the animosity persists. Though a truce or even a peace treaty may be negotiated, the Bible clearly predicts continued trouble and war between Egypt and Israel. Only the return of Jesus Christ will bring permanent peace.

Kings of the South

Chapter 11 of the Book of Daniel is a remarkable piece of prophecy. Remarkable because much of it, though future when written, has now been fulfilled, and thus we can test the accuracy of Daniel's words. Remarkable because we are given a detailed picture of some of the wars that are yet to be fought.

Ten times in this one chapter the title "King of the South" appears. It refers to Egypt's ruler, but not always to the same individual. It's like saying "President of the United States." Which president? There have been thirty-eight. Which King of the South? There have been six, all related to the Ptolemaic period of Egyptian history, and there is one more yet to come in the future.

The first one (Daniel 11:5) was Ptolemy I Soter (323–285 B.C.), who invaded Palestine in 320 B.C., marched to Jerusalem, but was scared off by the approach of Antigonus, the Greek general.

The second King of the South (mentioned in verse 6) was Ptolemy II Philadelphus (283–246 B.C.). Just as Daniel predicted, he gave his daughter Berenice to Antiochus II Theos on the condition that he divorce his actual wife, Laodice. This Antiochus did, but when Ptolemy died, he went back to his first love, Laodice, and for his trouble, was poisoned by her. She also killed Berenice and her son.

The third King of the South (mentioned in verses 7 to 9) was Ptolemy III Euergetes (246–221 B.C.), Berenice's brother, who attempted an invasion of Syria. News of an insurrection of Egypt forced him to return home, but not before he came away with "4000 talents of silver and 2500 precious vessels and images of the gods."

The fourth King of the South (mentioned in verse 11) was Ptolemy IV Philopator (221–204 B.C.), who reportedly had an army of 70,000 infantry, 5,000 cavalry, and 73 elephants!

He was succeeded by the fifth King of the South, his four-year-old son, Ptolemy V Epiphanes (203–181 B.C. and referred to in verse 15), who defeated Antiochus III ("the Great") but later suffered a crushing defeat by Antiochus. After this battle in 198 B.C. Palestine was transferred from the rule of the Ptolemys in Egypt back to the rule of the Seleucids in Syria.

The sixth King of the South was Ptolemy Philometor (181–145 B.C., mentioned in verse 15). He tried to recapture Palestine from Antiochus Epiphanes, but was chased back to Egypt and defeated just east of the Nile delta.

In the Middle

One thing stands out in this brief sketch of the Kings of the South. They were constantly battling with the kings of Syria. South versus North, with Palestine sandwiched in the middle. That's the way it was before Jesus appeared in human history, and that's the way it will be until He comes back again.

One more King of the South has yet to appear on the scene of history, and once more Palestine will find itself in the middle of the hostilities.

Antichrist, Front and Center

Enter Antichrist once again (Daniel 11:36), that great leader of United Europe. He is the one who will make the pact with Israel during the first part of that unique period of trouble that lies ahead. He is the one who will break the pact as easily as he made it and demand to be worshiped, while actually enthroning himself in the temple in Jerusalem. And he and his armies will do battle with the final King of the South.

Daniel describes Antichrist as a vile person. He will be insolent and self-centered, "doing as he pleases." He will "magnify himself above every god." He will blaspheme God (Revelation 13:6) and attempt to have himself worshiped in place of God (2 Thessalonians 2:4). He will say monstrous things against the true God, things no other man has ever dared to speak. He will be the world-champion blasphemer. And he will prosper in his wickedness until God destroys him.

He will have no respect for religion or religious heritage. He will be coarse, unkind, and cruel. His god will be the "god of fortresses." This striking phrase simply means that military activity will be his god, and he will worship it with all his wealth. He will scarcely be able to do otherwise, for war is expensive, and everything valuable will be prostrated to his god. All this is predicted in Daniel 11:37, 38.

We've Had the Preview

The world has already had a preview of Antichrist in the person of Antiochus IV (175–164 B.C.). History tells us about him and so did Daniel (11:21–35). Daniel introduced him as a "contemptible person," whose contemporaries knew him as a schemer and untrustworthy person. About 169 B.C. he added to his name the title Theos

Epiphanes, which means "God manifest." However, this was soon replaced by the nickname Epimanes, which means "madman." Though Antiochus wanted to be worshiped, he did not measure up to the character of the future Antichrist. Nor could he command exclusive worship as Antichrist will.

Antiochus also foreshadowed the intense persecution of the Jewish people which Antichrist will carry out in the future. In 170 B.C. Antiochus seized the temple treasury of Jerusalem in the name of Zeus, his god.

> And after that Antiochus had smitten Egypt, he returned again in the hundred forty and third year, and went up against Israel and Jerusalem with a great multitude, and entered proudly into the sanctuary, and took away the golden altar, and the candlestick of light, and all the vessels thereof, and the table of the shewbread and the pouring vessels, and the vials, and the censers of gold, and the veil, and the crowns, and the golden ornaments that were before the temple, all which he pulled off. He took also the silver and the gold, and the precious vessels: and he took the hidden treasurers which he found. And when he had taken all away, he went into his own land, having made a great massacre, and spoken very proudly.
>
> 1 Maccabees 1:20–24

But this was only the beginning of his sacrilege. Two years later he actually turned the temple into a Greek house of worship and profaned it by an utterly contemptible act. The historian Josephus described it this way:

> And when the king had built an idol altar upon God's altar, he slew swine upon it, and so offered a sacrifice neither according to the law, nor the Jewish religious worship in that country. He also compelled them to forsake the worship which they paid their own God, and to adore those whom he took to be gods; and made them build temples and raise idol altars, in every city and village, and offer swine upon them every day.
>
> Antiquities 7.5.4

In 164 B.C. the Jewish people, under the leadership of Judas the Maccabee, recaptured Jerusalem and cleansed the temple, restoring its proper rituals. The feast of Hanukkah (or Dedication), sometimes called the Festival of Lights, celebrates this momentous event.

Far worse than Antiochus will be Antichrist, who will lock horns with the last King of the South in that time of great tribulation that is coming.

Strange Bedfellows

Remember Magog from the last chapter? We learned that Magog is Russia, and that she will be allied with several other countries in an attempted blitz of Palestine. Ezekiel called her Magog. Daniel called her the King of the North. Ezekiel related that Magog will come from the extreme northern parts, making the title King of the North a fitting one indeed.

In the past, Kings of the South have all emerged from the territory of Egypt. And so it will be with the final one (Daniel 11:42, 43). Before A.D. 642 most Egyptians were members of the Coptic branch of Christianity, but today fewer than one in ten are Copts. More than 90 percent give allegiance to Islam, the Muslim faith introduced by the invaders from Arabia in A.D. 642, which teaches that Allah is the sole deity and Muhammad his prophet.

By contrast, the official religion of Russia is atheism. Atheism embraces no deity and no prophet. This very basic religious difference has prompted the Arab countries to keep Russia at arm's length, except in rare cases for diplomatic or military reasons. But there is coming a time when these two giant power blocs will unite in a great military campaign.

The Pincer Plan

A pincer is an instrument with two claws used to grab something. Russia, you remember, will want to grab Palestine. Though she will have six allies, she will need one more to form an effective pincer. None of the nations in the Arabian peninsula will be her ally. Ethiopia is in the Sudan, too far south of Palestine to be of much help. Libya is too far west. But the King of the South is situated perfectly: right on the southern doorstep of the land that is up for grabs. Russia will form the northern claw, Egypt the southern claw; put them together—strange alliance that it will be—and you have the pincer.

The attack will be launched on both fronts simultaneously. The King of the South will come up from Egypt. The King of the North will swoop down from Russia, through Turkey by land and across the Mediterranean by sea. The attack from the north will be an amphibious assault using horses and ships (Daniel 11:40).

The target: Palestine. But Antichrist will already have vested interests in Palestine, by virtue of the treaty which he will sign with Israel when that unique time of trouble begins. During the early years of the treaty, Antichrist will also be busy consolidating his empire in the West. His interests will be divided. And so the King of the North will seize the opportunity to invade Palestine. North and South will mount a simultaneous attack, Israel will cry for assistance, and Antichrist and his forces will come to her defense.

> And at the end time, the king of the South will collide with [Antichrist], and the king of the North will storm against him with chariots, with horsemen, and with many ships. . . .
>
> Daniel 11:40 NAS

Instant Cash

First, Antichrist will secure Palestine. "Many will fall," Daniel predicted, indicating that many Jews and invaders of the land will die. Then Antichrist will take on the King of the South and defeat the Egyptian army. While the King of the North continues to mass troops, Antichrist will chase the remnants of the army of the South back to Egypt. During a swift foray into Egypt he will loot, plunder, and seize the treasures of that country to further finance his own war efforts. With gold and silver the principal currencies of the day, he will gain tremendous wealth by plundering the rich museums in Egypt. You might call it instant cash, with no repayment plan.

Mopping Up

It appears that the first wave of attack by the King of the North will be repelled by Antichrist. It will take a little time for Russia to transport more troops to Palestine. The great distances will complicate the logistics. So Antichrist will feel that while in Egypt he has time to do some additional mopping up. He will attack Libya and Ethiopia and easily defeat them (Daniel 11:43).

You remember that Ethiopia and Libya are Allies No. 3 and No. 4 of Russia according to Ezekiel's forecast (Ezekiel 38:5). But geographically they are not tied to Russia and her allies in the north. As a result they will fall easy prey to Antichrist. If Russia's first thrust into Israel is turned back by Antichrist, then Russia will be forced to concentrate her efforts on bringing in additional men and equipment from the north. She won't be able to give much help to Sudan (Ethiopia) and Libya. Seeing his chance, Antichrist will capture these two countries while he is in Egypt. Instant cash from Egypt. Instant oil from Libya!

The League Beleaguered

Since its inception in 1945 the seven nations that form the Arab League have been beleaguered, not by an assault from nations outside the League but by internal discord. There is no logical reason for this. Their manpower is overwhelming; today their money could buy most American businesses. They share a common religion. They have a common enemy in Israel. But although they cooperate, they do not seem able to unite. When the King of the South attacks Israel, he may receive help from other Arab countries, but apparently they will not ally themselves together with Egypt. Listen to Daniel: "[Antichrist] will also enter [Palestine], and many countries will fall; but these will be rescued out of his hand: Edom, Moab and the foremost of the sons of Ammon" (11:41 NAS).

Where are Edom, Moab, and Ammon? Edom curves around the southern end of the Dead Sea. Moab lies to the east of the Dead Sea. Ammon occupies the land east of the Jordan River. Today this territory is the Hashemite Kingdom of Jordan. If Jordan were allied with Egypt, then Antichrist could not afford to let her escape. But he will not concern himself with Jordan as he sweeps south to capture Egypt, Sudan, and Libya.

The North Will Rise Again

Antichrist has staved off the first attack from the King of the North. He has, temporarily at least, planted himself securely in Israel. Now he turns his attention south and snaps off the southern arm of the pincer. While still engaged in the mopping-up operations in Africa, he hears "rumors from the East and the North" which alarm him (Daniel 11:44). What rumors? Reports from his intelligence sources that the King of the North is poised for another attack. In addition, the armies from the east are marching toward Palestine. The situation is extremely serious, so Antichrist turns back toward Palestine "with great wrath to destroy and annihilate many." Worldwide domination is literally within his grasp. The "god of fortresses" has blessed his war efforts so far. Will his god give him just one more victory?

God Helps the Ungodly

The blitz begins. The King of the North arrives in Israel. The Kings of the East are fast approaching. Antichrist amasses his forces which have temporarily been diverted into Egypt, and streaks toward Palestine. The odds seem stacked against him, for now he must face two powerful armies. The critical question is: Will he have to face them both at once, or will he be able to take them on one at a time? Since the armies from the East have not yet actually arrived in Israel, perhaps he can defeat the King of the North quickly, then take on the Kings of the East.

Never in Antichrist's wildest dreams could he have predicted what happens next: The God of Israel comes to his aid! Inconceivable, you say. After all, Antichrist is god, at least in his own mind. And if he serves any god at all, it is the god of war. But no Antichrist or King of the North can control the forces of nature. Only the true God can do that.

And control it He will, at precisely the right moment for Antichrist. Do you remember what Ezekiel prophesied? God will cause a great earthquake in the land of Israel, and will send fire upon the armies of the King of the North (Ezekiel 38:19, 20, 22 and 39:6).

> . . . I shall rain on him, and on his troops, and on the many peoples who are with him, a torrential rain with hailstones, fire, and brimstone.
>
> Ezekiel 38:22 NAS

Can you imagine Antichrist's glee? One enemy force totally destroyed—and he didn't lose a single man or expend an ounce of gold doing it. Can't you see him and his generals congratulating each other on their good fortune? And that's how he will view this fortuitous turn of events. As good fortune. Good luck. A golden opportunity to take over the entire world.

But we know better. God will destroy the King of the North, not because He is in league with Antichrist, but because He is in control of all the events of history: past, present, and future. He will allow

Antichrist to capture Russia's allies in the south: Sudan and Libya; but He Himself will personally wipe out Russia and her northern allies. Why? I repeat: not because He is seeking to promote Antichrist, but because He desires to punish the King of the North. Ezekiel saw it as God's wrath blazing against the hordes of the North so that the nations of the world, including those controlled by Antichrist, will know that God is the Lord. That's a hard way to have to learn the lesson, but it seems the world refuses to learn it any other way.

Any More Worlds to Conquer?

One last hurdle remains: the Kings of the East. Whoever conquers them rules the world, and Antichrist knows it. Antichrist may be a great military genius, but he will flunk as a student of theology! He won't learn his lesson from God's destroying the King of the North. So God will have to show Antichrist once again who really rules this world. The classroom will be a place called Armageddon.

Some Sure Things

Let's summarize and make some predictions.

First, Egypt will continue as an important world power. If there is an eclipse it will be only temporary, and she will rise again to prominence.

Second, Egypt and Israel will continue to be enemies. No peace treaty will be able to erase their basic enmity, which will erupt again in those future days of great tribulation.

Third, Jordan will go it alone, maintaining more of a neutral position rather than aligning with one of the power blocs.

Fourth, Egypt will be conquered during that future period of great tribulation.

Fifth, Egypt will experience future national glory surpassing anything in its ancient past. Read on.

Future Egypt

Encyclopedias almost always contain a section entitled "Ancient Egypt." But nowhere do we ever read about "Future Egypt." Except in the Bible. And it has much to say about the coming glory of Egypt.

Muslim Egypt will one day be converted to worshiping the true God! Nothing could seem more impossible today, but listen to the prophet Isaiah: ". . . the Egyptians will know the Lord in that day. They will even worship with sacrifice and offering, and will make a vow to the Lord and perform it" (19:21 NAS). When will this happen? When Jesus Christ returns to deliver Egypt and the world from the tyranny of Antichrist. Not only the land of Israel, but all nations will need His deliverance. And then Egyptians, along with many others, will recognize the true God and Savior of the world.

When men's hearts change, their relationships with others also change. Egypt, after her conversion, will live at peace with those who were once her sworn enemies. Two of these age-old enemies are Assyria and Israel. As long ago as 680 B.C. Assyria imperiled Egypt. Invasions of Egyptian territory were successfully launched by Assyrian leaders Esarhaddon and Ashurbanipal. Today Iraq stands on part of the old Assyrian empire. And although Iraq and Egypt are allied in their common struggle against Israel today, in that coming day they will both enjoy peace with Israel. Egypt on the southwest, Israel in the middle, and Assyria on the northeast will live together in a peaceful triple union! Travel and communication will be unhindered. The natural water boundaries separating the countries will be removed. Isaiah, twenty-seven hundred years ago, predicted that the tongue of the Red Sea, the northwestern finger that leads to the Suez, would one day be destroyed. He also predicted that the people would be able to cross over the Euphrates River on the eastern boundary of Palestine—dry-shod! Read Isaiah 11:15 and see for yourself.

Imagine—"the United States of Egypt, Israel, and Assyria," with all its citizens worshiping the true God. That's future Egypt, and only God can accomplish such a miracle.

> In that day there will be a highway from Egypt to Assyria, and the Assyrians will come into Egypt and the Egyptians into Assyria, and the Egyptians will worship with the Assyrians. In that day Israel will be the third party with Egypt and Assyria, a blessing in the midst of the earth, whom the Lord of hosts has blessed, saying, "Blessed is Egypt My people, and Assyria the work of My hands, and Israel My inheritance."
>
> Isaiah 19:23–25 NAS

That will be *some* news from the Nile!

7

The Great Leap From the East

The most monumental political movement in history, involving one-fourth of all humanity, has unfolded before the eyes of this generation in the emergence of a new powerhouse in the east: China.

China, the third-largest country in the world, is exceeded in size only by Russia and Canada. It sprawls over one-fifth of Asia and is slightly larger than the United States. During the quarter century since the People's Republic was founded on October 1, 1949, China has catapulted into world prominence. Peking's leadership role in world affairs, a role which now includes a seat on the UN Security Council, has been firmly established. Indeed, the Great Leap Forward has startled and amazed the world.

China, along with other nations of the East, will play a prominent role in the drama that unfolds in that unique era of trouble that lies ahead. You remember that when Antichrist mops up in Egypt and Africa "rumors from the East and the North will alarm him" (Daniel 11:44). His intelligence agents will report that armies from the Russian confederation are poised for attack again; in addition, a massive attack from the Kings of the East appears imminent.

About nineteen hundred years ago John, Jesus' "beloved disciple," predicted some of the details of that attack from the East. And contemporary events in that part of the world ought to alert us to the nearness of that coming war.

It's Dawning on Us
Here's what John foresaw:

> The sixth angel poured out his bowl on the great river Euphrates, and its water was dried up to prepare the way for the kings from the east.
>
> Revelation 16:12 NIV

Who are these "kings from the east"? Literally, the phrase in the original language of the New Testament means "kings of the rising of the sun."

Look at the national flag of Japan, where a round red sun stands out on a surrounding white field. Japan is called the Land of the Rising Sun. The Japanese people call their country Nippon, which means Source of the Sun. One hundred years ago Japan was isolated from the rest of the world. In 1853–54 U.S. Commander Matthew Perry forced two Japanese ports to open to U.S. trade. Learning quickly the ways of the West, the Japanese turned their country into a great economic and military power. Her defeat in World War II and surrender in 1945 left Japan a shambles. Though cities lay in ruins and industries were shattered, in a single decade Japan emerged again as a great industrial nation. Today, more than 100 million people share this prosperity.

China and Japan, two new great eastern powers in this generation. It's beginning to dawn on us that something important is unfolding before our eyes.

Evaporate, Euphrates!

One of the longest rivers in western Asia, the Euphrates flows approximately 1,780 miles from the mountains of Turkey to the Persian Gulf. (By comparison, the Mississippi River is about 2,350 miles long.) From 300 to 1,200 yards wide and 10 to 30 feet deep, the Euphrates is scarcely fordable at any point along its banks or at any time during the year. It has always formed a formidable boundary between those who lived east and west of it, and represents the eastern boundary of the land God promised to Abraham and his descendants (Genesis 15:18). The main crossing was controlled in ancient times by the famous fortress city of Carchemish, sixty-three miles northeast of what is today Aleppo, Syria.

Whatever natural barriers exist now to prevent an easy crossing of the river will one day be demolished. Earthquakes and upheavals will cause tremendous topographical changes during those coming years of great tribulation. The rocky cliffs and banks which make the Euphrates unfordable will be leveled. But the river itself, wider than a football field in places, will still make it difficult for a large army to cross. Once again God will intervene. He will supernaturally dry up the Euphrates.

Imagine the scene. The armies of the Kings of the East are drawing near to the Euphrates on their march to Palestine. Plans are being made for the crossing of this final barrier to the Holy Land. Amphibious vehicles are ordered to the front. Pontoon bridges are frantically being prepared. Suddenly, before the very eyes of those on the front lines, the water just disappears. Word is flashed back to the field commanders. It can't be true. This has never happened in the history of warfare. Quick reconnaissance verifies the reports. Officers and enlisted men alike are jubilant. This will cut days off their planned schedule and give the Kings of the East an unexpected advantage over Antichrist and his armies. Their intelligence has carefully tracked the movements of the Russian alliance and Antichrist's forces. And now they will be in Palestine ahead of schedule. Defeat of Antichrist seems assured. Drinks all around! The Euphrates has evaporated!

Let Loose, Euphrates!

Jesus taught that demons can reside in people and pigs (Matthew 8:28, 32), and they can be kept in rivers, too! Today, apparently, the Euphrates imprisons four powerful demons who are being kept there until the invasion from the east begins. Their job is to incite this mighty army at the end of that period of great tribulation. Powerful and fierce as demons are, God is more powerful, and He will restrain their activity until He chooses to let them loose. John said they would be held in check until "the hour, the day, the month, and the year" of this invasion (Revelation 9:15).

Their work parallels their character: demonic and horrible. They will destroy one-third of the population of the world. How will they do this? By inciting an army of 200 million to perform unspeakable atrocities.

War has always been terrible, but modern warfare accentuates the horror. Front-line action halfway around the world is instantly brought into our homes via TV. But demon-inspired war will be the epitome of horror. And that is what's in store for the world when those four demon-generals are released from their Euphrates prison.

The U.S. in Arms

The population of the United States is about 250 million. If four out of every five people in this country were pressed into military service, the total would equal that of the immense army of the nations of the East. Just think: only one in every five people left in the United

States, while all the others wage war. That, by comparison, is the enormous size of the armies of the East.

But how will the eastern nations amass such an army? As long ago as 1965 China alone claimed to have a home militia (consisting of men and women under training) numbering 200 million (*Time,* May 21, 1965). Undoubtedly this includes many who would not be thrown into a full-scale war, but it is startling that this figure is the same as John foresaw nineteen hundred years ago—when the total population of the world was not even 200 million! It takes some courage to be a prophet! It doesn't take much insight for us who are living today to see the possibilities of fulfillment of this prophecy.

But China won't furnish all the manpower. Other eastern nations will join the alliance. While it is true that the constitution of Japan prohibits the use of war as a political weapon, not even a casual observer of history would doubt that such provision might easily be violated!

The Giant Comes to Life

Technologically, China has come to life during the past decade. She exploded her first atomic bomb in 1964, and tested her first H-bomb two and a half years later. Intercontinental missile capacity is now a reality in China, placing the United States and Europe within striking distance. Her first guided missile armed with a nuclear warhead was successfully test-fired as early as 1966.

But in addition to technological know-how, a successful war machine must have enormous economic resources. And China has them. In the last twenty-five years China's output of grain has more than doubled; coal production has increased tenfold; and oil output has skyrocketed nearly 400 percent! In 1973 China scored a significant economic victory by becoming an oil exporter instead of an oil importer. Proved reserves of around 20 billion barrels (vs. 35 billion for the United States and 132 billion for Saudi Arabia) will provide necessary foreign exchange earnings for China. In 1974 alone Peking exported 30.5 million barrels of crude oil to Japan. This was an increase of 430 percent over the previous year's exports and was used to great political advantage. Strong political and economic links are being forged between the two nations.

Annual increases in grain production provide for China's continually increasing population, with a surplus even left for export. Two years ago China began to buy whole industrial plants from Japan and

Western Europe. Increasing foreign trade is making China an important customer and supplier in the world economic community. Foreign trade is up from $1.2 billion in 1950 to $17 billion in 1975.

The manpower of the nations of the East make a 200-million-man army feasible; their industrial muscles are flexed to supply such an army.

Nuclear Holocaust

When East meets West in battle, the outcome will be swift and predictable: carnage on a worldwide scale. One-third of all those still living on the earth will be destroyed in the holocaust (Revelation 9:15). The armies, too, will be destroyed. Listen to the ancient prophet Zechariah as he describes the horrible scene:

> Now this will be the plague with which the Lord will strike all the peoples who have gone to war against Jerusalem; their flesh will rot while they stand on their feet, and their eyes will rot in their sockets, and their tongue will rot in their mouth.
>
> Zechariah 14:12 NAS

John predicted that the third of the population killed in the hostilities would die as a result of "fire and smoke and brimstone" (Revelation 9:17, 18). Couple this with Zechariah's description, and it is hard to avoid the picture of atomic warfare. Any nuclear arms limitation treaty will only restrain the use of nuclear weapons, not remove their threatening presence. Stockpiles of nuclear devices will still remain to be used in these final battles.

East Meets West

This will be the final showdown between East and West: the Kings of the East in a fight to the finish with Antichrist and the West. But suddenly, a strange new enemy will appear on the scene. From what direction will he arrive? Not from the North (God will have destroyed the Russian alliance by this time); not from the South (Antichrist will have conquered Egypt by then); not from the East or West (all their forces will already be committed to the battle); but from above. Suddenly, at the height of the conflagration, the King of Kings will appear in the sky, followed by His heavenly armies, and will descend to the earth.

Instant Allies

Abruptly the East-West enmity will vanish, and a new alliance will quickly be cemented. A common enemy often produces strange bed-fellows. Former foes will become fast friends as East and West realize that they are facing the King of Kings.

This is Armageddon. The combatants: the armies of the earth (what's left of them) and the armies of heaven. The place: Palestine. The time: at the end of that seven-year time of terrible trouble. The outcome: rebellion quashed and Christ victorious.

The Crystal Ball

If the end is near, what may we expect to see developing in the immediate future?

Expect Japan to continue as a leading industrial nation of the world. Temporary setbacks may result because of energy shortages, but they will be just that: temporary.

Watch for the awakening giant, China, to flex her military and economic muscles.

Remember that in the final lineup of nations, Russia and China will square off on opposite sides. Though there may be temporary détente between these two great powers, ultimately they will find themselves in different power blocs. Ideological differences, economic and military competition, or a combination of these factors may be necessary to bring this alignment. But come it will!

8

A Bloodbath for Israel

"He who touches Israel touches the apple of God's eye." That's what the prophet Zechariah said twenty-four hundred years ago. And it's still true.

New York, headquarters for the United Nations. Geneva, center of numerous worldwide organizations. Tokyo, largest city in the world. Moscow, nerve center of communism. Peking, mysterious city of the Orient. Jerusalem, shaky capital of a tiny nation.

But Jerusalem is the city to watch. Jerusalem is the place where the history of this age will climax.

Why are the Jewish people and the city of Jerusalem so important? Because they present a problem to the world that no one has ever been able to resolve. Dictators have tried in vain to destroy the Jews. While the dictators come and go, the Jews remain with us. Hitler liquidated 6 million Jews during World War II, but almost that many are still alive today in the United States alone. Less than one hundred years ago there were only about 24,000 Jewish people in Palestine. Today the number approaches 3 million. The government of Israel predicts that by 1990 there will be 4.2 million Jews residing in Israel. No person or nation can hope to destroy the apple of God's eye.

And the Jewish problem will persist right to the end.

Say That Again, Zechariah
Listen to that prophet Zechariah again: "Behold, I am going to make Jerusalem a cup that causes reeling to all the peoples around . . . . I will make Jerusalem a heavy stone for all the peoples; all who lift it will be severely injured" (Zechariah 12:2, 3 NAS).

Why should the world be so bothered about a relatively insignificant people like the Jews? Because God chose them to enjoy a very special relationship with Himself, and because God promised certain blessings to the Jews, blessings which they have yet to experience.

Before 1948 the thirteen million Jews in this world were living peacefully in nations scattered around the world. About half a million resided in Palestine, living with and among their Arab neighbors. Suddenly, Great Britain announced that she would no longer be responsible for Palestine, a territory mandated to her by the defunct League of Nations. The scramble was on. On May 14, 1948, David Ben Gurion read the Declaration of Independence announcing the establishment of the State of Israel. On May 15 the Kingdom of Jordan officially came into existence. When the armistice was finally signed, Israel emerged with eight thousand square miles of territory in what she had always considered her homeland. Suddenly, the attention of the world was focused on a single tiny nation. And ever since 1948 the UN, the United States, Russia, Europe, and the Arab nations have all concerned themselves with the fate and fortunes of Israel.

It Was God's Choice

God sovereignly chose Israel. Not because the Jews deserved the honor any more than any other people, but because the Lord loved them (Deuteronomy 7:8). And He is not through with them yet, either. "God has not cast away His people" (Romans 11:2).

Promises, Promises

God promised them something, too. He promised to make the Jewish people, the descendants of Abraham, into a great nation (Genesis 12:2; 13:16; 15:5). He also promised to bless those who were kind to the Jews and curse those who treated them harshly (Genesis 12:3), an inviolable law that has been in operation ever since.

But the most intriguing promise made to the Jewish people concerns a piece of real estate. Abraham and his descendants were promised the land "from the river of Egypt to the great river, the river Euphrates" (Genesis 15:18), and this land was given to them "for an everlasting possession" (Genesis 17:8). But the fact is, they have never possessed it. So either God went back on His promise, or the Jews will yet possess it sometime in the future. There are no other options.

What Rivers?

The boundaries of that promised land are two rivers. The Euphrates is specified, leaving no question about the eastern boundary. But there is some debate over the identification of the "River of Egypt." Some think it refers to a stream called the Wadi-el-Arish, not far from Gaza. Others think it clearly means the Nile. There are two different words used in the Hebrew language to indicate a stream of water. One refers to a wadi, the other a river. The word used in this promise is the one for river. A wadi is a stream that is full only after it rains and is dry the rest of the year; a river is a stream that flows the year around. During the 1967 War Israel pushed beyond the Wadi-el-Arish but stopped at Suez, short of the Nile. In 1974 she withdrew from the Suez Canal, and moved back toward the wadi. Back and forth, back and forth. But someday all the land from the Euphrates to the Nile will be in Jewish hands. God keeps His promises.

Persecution, Persecution

One of the most improbable facts of world history is the survival of the Jewish people. Israel's precarious existence is a testimony to God's faithfulness in keeping His promises. He has said that if the fixed order of the sun, moon, and stars by day and by night ceases, "Then the offspring of Israel also shall cease from being a nation before Me forever" (*see* Jeremiah 31:36 NAS). So, every time you feel the sun's warmth and every time you see the moon and stars, you can be sure the Jewish people will survive. God has given His word.

But Israel's history has not been an easy one. In 722 B.C. Samaria was destroyed and the flower of the Northern Kingdom was carried off by the Assyrians. In the 600s B.C. the rest of the populace was hauled off to Babylon. During the four hundred years that elapsed between the close of the Old Testament and the opening of the New Testament, tens of thousands of Jews were slaughtered or sold into slavery. On one occasion Antiochus Epiphanes (who ruled from 175–164 B.C.) killed forty thousand Jews and sold forty thousand more into slavery. The reason: Rumor had spread that Antiochus was dead, and the Jews had begun to celebrate prematurely.

When Rome was in the process of conquering Palestine during the years leading up to A.D. 70, many more Jews were slaughtered. In A.D. 68, twenty thousand were killed in Caesarea, and in a single day ten thousand more had their throats cut by the people of Damascus. When the temple in Jerusalem was finally destroyed in A.D. 70, some estimate that as many as six hundred thousand Jews were massacred. One historian estimates that during the years A.D. 66 to 70 more than a million Jews lost their lives.

But the Roman persecution was not over. When the Emperor Hadrian (A.D. 117-138) turned Jerusalem into a Roman city and built a temple to Zeus on the site of the temple to Israel's Lord, the Jews predictably revolted. The Romans then destroyed 985 towns in Palestine and killed 580,000 men. Many more were sold into slavery.

The Crusades, which tried to recapture the holy places in Palestine from the Muslims, exterminated many Jews in Europe. Even the English and the French, as late as the thirteenth century, wiped out entire Jewish communities in their countries. And while Columbus was discovering America, Jews were being expelled from nearly all of western Europe. Hitler added to this awful record by exterminating more than six million Jews.

But the worst bloodbath in Jewish history is yet to come.

Two Down and One to Go

Three times in Israel's history the Jews have left the promised land. Twice they have returned. That means there's one return still to come.

The first departure from Palestine began when Joseph's brothers sold him into slavery, landing him in Egypt. Eventually his father Jacob's entire family of seventy persons joined Joseph because of famine in Palestine. But God produced a great deliverer in Moses, who led the Jews out of Egypt and back to Palestine. Moses' successor, Joshua, was promised that same land: ". . . even as far as the great river, the river Euphrates . . . and as far as the Great Sea toward the setting of the sun, will be your territory" (Joshua 1:4 NAS).

The second departure from Palestine was involuntary. God had warned His people that if they wanted blessing and peace they would have to keep His laws. But true to human nature, the Jewish people did not listen. Instead, they took the law into their own hands. They worshiped idols instead of the true God. They disobeyed specific commands, such as not permitting their land to lie fallow every seventh year so that it might recover and produce the needed crops year by year. For 490 years they disobeyed. Many must have said, "See, we're getting away with our sin. God doesn't notice." Maybe some even said, "God is dead." But all the time God was very much alive, and finally the situation got so bad that there was only one thing left for God to do: punish the people severely. So in 721 B.C. the great power Assyria took ten of the twelve tribes of Israel into captivity. A little more than a hundred years later Babylon, conqueror of Assyria, marched away with the remaining two tribes.

For seventy years the Jews were slaves in Babylon. But then in 539 B.C. Cyrus, King of Persia, decreed that they could return to Palestine if they wished. About fifty thousand of them made the arduous six-month trip back to the promised land, traversing over 900 miles of rugged terrain to reach their homeland. They completed the rebuilding of their temple in 516 B.C. but did not finish the walls of the city until 445 B.C. This was their second return.

The years passed. Greece replaced Persia as the number one world empire with Alexander's triumph at Issus in 333 B.C. In the first century B.C. Alexander's successors in the Near East lost out to Rome. Herod's temple replaced the one the returnees had built when they came back from Babylon. Jesus Christ lived and died.

Then came the awful Roman bloodbath in Palestine which climaxed in A.D. 70. The Jewish people were driven from their promised land and scattered throughout the world. Nineteen long centuries slowly passed, and only in recent years have they begun to return.

Enter Zionism

Not until the twentieth century has there been any move on the part of the Jewish people to return to Palestine.

The first Zionist Congress was held in Basel, Switzerland, in 1897. Theodor Herzl was the leader. The goal was "to create for the Jewish people a home in Palestine secured by public law." The movement was basically political, not religious, in nature.

Progress was slow. In 1914 only 85,000 Jews lived in Palestine, among a total population of 700,000. But then came a giant step forward in the Balfour Declaration. In order to gain the support of the Jewish people in the first World War, Arthur J. Balfour, British Foreign Secretary, issued a declaration on November 2, 1917, in which he said: "His Majesty's Government views with favour the establishment in Palestine of a national home for the Jewish people, and will use their best endeavours to facilitate the achievement of this object, it being clearly understood that nothing shall be done which may prejudice the civil and religious rights of existing non-Jewish communities in Palestine, or the rights and political status enjoyed by Jews in any other country."

This Declaration gave Zionism its long-awaited chance, and opened the door for larger and larger numbers of Jews to settle in Palestine.

Jew, Go Home

This influx of Jewish settlers did not make the Arab residents of Palestine happy. They wanted the Jews to go home. The Jews, on the other hand, thought that was precisely what they were doing.

The Arab League was formed in 1945. On November 29, 1947, the UN proposed a partitioning of Palestine into a Jewish and an Arab state, making Jerusalem an international city under UN control. The Arabs flatly rejected the partition.

What Was That, Joel?

We really know very little about the obscure Old Testament prophet named Joel. He probably prophesied about 830 B.C., eight centuries before Christ, and twenty-seven centuries before the UN partition of Palestine in 1947. Hear then what he said in the name of the Lord God of Israel: "I will also gather all nations . . . and will judge them there for my people and for my heritage, Israel, whom they have scattered among the nations, and have parted my land" (Joel 3:2). God knew twenty-seven centuries beforehand that the land would be partitioned.

United Jerusalem

War broke out between the Jews and Arabs when the British withdrew their supervision of Palestine in May 1948. The uneasy armistice of 1949 lasted for eighteen years until the Six-Day War of 1967.

The most important Jewish victory of that war was the capture of the old city of Jerusalem. Many tourists remember the two Jerusalems that existed up to that time. The new city on the west belonged to Israel, the old walled city and its suburbs on the east belonged to Jordan. Tourists were permitted a single one-way crossing from one city to the other. Many travelers made that crossing of no-man's-land at the so-called Mandelbaum Gate. In 1967 the city was united. Public utilities were quickly integrated, streets were joined, and no-man's-land was completely erased. Less than a year later the *Jerusalem Post* headline read: "600,000 See 20th Birthday Fete in United Jerusalem."

History Prewritten

The third return appears to have begun. Three departures, three returns. Almost-forgotten prophecies are beginning to be fulfilled before our eyes.

Isaiah wrote these words 2,600 years ago: "And it shall come to pass in that day, that the Lord shall set his hand again the second time to recover the remnant of his people who shall be left. . . . He shall assemble the outcasts of Israel, and gather together the dispersed of Judah from the four corners of the earth (Isaiah 11:11, 12).

A century later Jeremiah wrote on behalf of the Lord: "I will bring them again into their land that I gave unto their fathers" (Jeremiah 16:15 KJV.)

About the same time, Ezekiel also spoke for the Lord, saying: "I will take you from among the heathen, and gather you out of all countries, and will bring you into your own land" (Ezekiel 36:24 KJV).

This third return will be the final one. Israel will be gathered, never to scatter again. The prophet Amos described it this way: "I will bring again the captivity of my people of Israel, and they shall build the waste cities, and inhabit them; and they shall plant vineyards, and drink the wine thereof; they shall also make gardens, and eat the fruit of them. And I will plant them upon their land, and they shall no more be pulled up out of their land which I have given them, saith the Lord thy God" (Amos 9:14, 15 KJV).

Jacob's Trouble

This road to glory will not be an easy one. Before the Jewish people can experience the completion of their final return, when they will live safely and securely in the land, there must come what the Bible calls the time of Jacob's trouble.

Abraham, Isaac, Jacob: the first and greatest names in the line of the Jewish people. Jacob's trouble is that coming period of distress described by Jesus as He spoke to His disciples on the Mount of Olives. Jeremiah labeled it "Jacob's trouble" and said it would be unique in all history (Jeremiah 30:7). Jesus called it a period of unprecedented tribulation (Matthew 24:21). This will be the time of Israel's greatest bloodbath.

But it won't begin that way. This seven-year period of unparalleled distress will begin with Israel at the negotiating table, still seeking that elusive dream of peace and security.

What in particular will bring Israel to the negotiating table? The answer is simple: Jerusalem.

In the early years following the declaration of independence of Israel, foreign countries had their embassies in Tel Aviv. They may have kept representatives in Jerusalem but the principal embassies were in Tel Aviv. The reason was obvious; Jerusalem was a divided city only partly controlled by Israel. But more important than that was the sensitive problem of maintaining the shaky relations between Israel and the Arab nations surrounding her. Foreign governments avoided any hint of endorsing Israel's claim to Jerusalem as her capital city by placing their embassies outside Jerusalem.

But to the leaders and people of Israel there was never any question about the status and importance of Jerusalem. "Jerusalem is our capital city," was their cry, a cry raised often and loud during those first years of Jewish independence. There was never any question in Israeli minds, for they immediately located their parliament in Jerusalem. To be sure, it was housed in temporary headquarters, not in the fine building it currently occupies; but the important point to every Israeli was that the Knesset, the parliament, was meeting in Jerusalem. Jerusalem was their capital city, and they wanted the whole world to know it.

In 1967 one of the most momentous events in all Jewish history took place. For the first time since Jerusalem was captured by the Romans in A.D. 70 the city was returned to Jewish control. For almost 2,000 years others had ruled the sacred city. Since the 1948 war of independence, Israeli citizens had been barred from those sections of the city which Jordan controlled. And *the* most important sacred site for Jewish people was in Arab hands. The temple area was inaccessible to Jewish citizens of Israel. But in 1967 all that changed. In the Six-Day War Israel captured Jerusalem, returning the temple area and the Wailing Wall to Jewish control. It was a day of great rejoicing. Every Jewish leader hurried to the Wailing Wall to offer prayers of thanksgiving for the recapture of the city.

One of the first government actions was to enlarge the area in front of the Wailing Wall. Houses were literally swept away to make a large plaza where thousands of people could gather on holy occasions.

Yes, Jerusalem is the key that unlocks the mystery of why Israel, proud and fiercely independent, will sign a treaty with Antichrist.

Successful as they were in capturing Jerusalem, Jewish leaders since 1967 have found no way to regain access to any part of the temple area except the Wailing Wall. And that area she must have. Solomon built his magnificent temple there (2 Chronicles 3:1, 2). Those who returned from captivity in Babylon also built their temple there (Ezra 3:10). Herod's beautiful and spectacular temple was also on that site (Matthew 24:1, 2). And the hope of the Jews is that another temple will rise again on that same site: a temple in which they can practice their ancient rituals; a temple that will be the center of Judaism; a temple in Jerusalem that will serve as a rallying point for Jews scattered throughout the world.

But something stands in the way of that dream.

It's called Al-Haramesh-Sharif, the Dome of the Rock, a beautiful golden-domed, octagonally shaped Muslim mosque. Built in A.D. 691, the Dome is second only to the city of Mecca as a holy place for Muslim people.

But during the tribulation days there will be a Jewish temple in Jerusalem and presumably on this very site. Jesus said so (Matthew 24:15), and Paul said so (2 Thessalonians 2:4). John also saw it in his visions (Revelation 11:2). Maybe the mosque will be destroyed by natural means. Perhaps the temple will stand beside a closed mosque. But there will be a temple, and the Jewish people will once again practice their religion in it. Antichrist himself will see to that!

Protector Turned Traitor

After three and one-half years of protecting Israel, Antichrist will turn traitor. The protector of Israel will become the persecutor of Israel. The intensity of this persecution and the urgent need for evacuating Jerusalem as quickly as possible have already been described in chapter 2. Antichrist will desecrate the temple by bringing some unholy thing into the holy place. We know what that unholy thing will be: It will be Antichrist himself. He will sit in the holy place and demand to be worshiped.

Remember the Preview

This happened once before. Antiochus IV, a Syrian ruler and one of the successors of Alexander the Great, tried to introduce Greek civilization into all the territories he ruled, including Palestine. He forbade the practice of Judaism. Anyone caught observing the Sabbath or circumcising a child was to be killed. The years of his reign, 175–164 B.C., brought some of the darkest hours in Israel's history. The climax of this terrible time came in 167 B.C., when he profaned the temple in Jerusalem by offering pigs on the altar.

But horrible as this desecration was for the Jewish people, it was only a preview of the time when Antichrist will place himself in the temple and demand to be worshiped. Those who refuse will be singled out, hunted down, and killed.

When Antichrist must be away from Jerusalem in order to attend affairs of state, he will leave an image of himself in the temple to be worshiped. He will also leave behind a lieutenant who will see to it that the people worship the image (Revelation 13:14).

Caught in the Middle

In addition to the religious squeeze, however, there will also be a political squeeze, for the country of Israel is strategically located. Antichrist will have the west behind him, politically and geographically. If he and his armies can control Israel, they will be able to defend themselves against invaders from all other points of the compass. And come they will, from all directions. Armies from the north, south, and east will attack, and Jerusalem will be caught in the middle.

What Did You Say, Zechariah?

"I will gather all the nations against Jerusalem to battle, and the city will be captured, the houses plundered, the women ravished, and half of the city exiled, but the rest of the people will not be cut off from the city" (Zechariah 14:2 NAS). The final battle of this age will center both at Armageddon (in the north of Israel) and in Jerusalem (in the center of the country). Once again Jerusalem will be trampled by armies, but this time it will be the armies of the world.

How Will It All End?

It will take someone more powerful than Antichrist to stop his advance. It will take armies more powerful than those the nations of the world can muster to subdue his forces. Who will do it? Jesus Christ and His heavenly armies. Zechariah saw it all twenty-four hundred years ago. Listen:

> Then the Lord will go forth and fight against those nations.
> His feet will stand on the Mount of Olives. . . .
> And the Lord will be king over all the earth. . . .
> There shall be no more destruction. . . .
> Jerusalem shall be safely inhabited.
>
> Zechariah 14:3, 4, 9, 11

> Pray for the peace of Jerusalem:
> "May they prosper who love you."
>
> Psalms 122:6   NAS

9

The Devil Makes Them Do It

The devil is big business today.

A few years ago it was estimated that 10,000 full-time and 175,000 part-time astrologers were practicing in America.

The astrology boom in France rakes in $650 million a year and supports half a million astrologers.

Spiritualism in Brazil has been called the country's fastest-growing cult.

As many as six thousand witches meet regularly in Britain.

Witchcraft generates a multimillion-dollar industry in America and publishes its own journal called the *Occult Trade Review.* Its half-dozen publishing houses turn out books like *The Stock Market and Witchcraft* and *Sexual Power Through Witchcraft.* In 1971 it was estimated that there were more than eighty thousand white witches in America. One Christian leader declared that there are more war-locks in Germany than Protestant pastors, more in France than practicing physicians.

Add to this all the tarot cards, astrology packets, Ouija boards, and occult bumper stickers that are sold every day, and the totals are staggering!

In Academe, Too

Courses on various aspects of the occult appear regularly in many university catalogs. Even high schools now offer such studies. Big business spends some of its profits for research into parapsychology. *Business Week* (January 26, 1974) reported that:

The National Institute of Mental Health has granted Brooklyn's Maimonides Medical Center funds for ESP tests;

NASA has financed a Stanford Research Institute program to teach ESP skills to NASA personnel;

Bell Telephone Laboratory scientists are working in the fields of telepathy and clairvoyance.

The devil is big business and he is serious business.

Satan's Little Helpers

The idea of a personal devil and active demons shocks our twentieth century sensibilities. But why? Who doesn't have that "feeling" that there's a sinister spirit abroad in the world? And besides, has anyone penned an authoritative book entitled *A Guide to All the Creatures in the Universe?* Could anyone? God can, and has, in the Bible. And since the Bible has proved itself true on other subjects, we ought to listen to what it says about the devil and his demons.

Satan does not fight alone. Demons are his cohorts in rebellion. Both Satan and the demons belong to the category of creatures we know as angels, only they are rebellious angels. They plotted to usurp the dominion that rightfully belongs to God and man. So when Jesus Christ begins to quell their rebellion by opening the seals on the scroll which is His deed to rule the world, we would expect the devil and his army of demons to fight with all their might. During the coming days of great tribulation they will muster all their resources against world leaders, against nations, and finally against Jesus Christ Himself. Here's how it will happen.

Satan, Ph.D.

Satan (another name for the devil, meaning "opponent") has the distinction of being the most intelligent creature in all the universe. There are two reasons for this: First, God made him that way, and second, he has learned a lot by living so long. To be sure, he employs that great mind for his own purposes, and this superintelligence makes him a formidable foe.

Furthermore, Satan is an efficient administrator. His goals have been carefully thought out; he has organized the demons better than any corporation has organized its employees; he knows how to be flexible in adapting his strategy to changing circumstances.

The Rev. Satan, Ph.D.

Satan's knowledge of religion would qualify him for ordination in almost any church. You remember that Jesus warned of coming pseudosaviors. Satan will be the force in back of them, and through them he will promote his own system of theology. Listen to what the apostle Paul said about that:

> The Spirit says clearly that in later times some will abandon
> the faith and follow deceiving spirits and things taught by

demons. Such teachings come through hypocritical liars, whose consciences have been seared as with a hot iron. They forbid people to marry and order them to abstain from certain foods. . . .

1 Timothy 4:1–3 NIV

Here demons are not cast in the role we usually assign them as appealing to people's lustful and baser desires. Instead, they battle for men's minds, seeking to teach their leader's system of religious doctrine. And they do this through human beings so that it all looks very normal and natural. Therefore, pulpits, not honky-tonks, and religious rallies, not dives, will form their base of operations.

Article 1

But what do demons teach? They teach salvation by human effort, even emphasizing self-denial as a way of life for their followers. Abstaining from marriage and from eating certain foods—these things tend to make the devotees feel that they are somehow earning their own salvation by their ascetic lives. And when a man senses no need for outside help, he finds it easy and logical to reject any offer of salvation from Jesus Christ. In reality, Jesus said that only one kind of work is of any value: "The work of God is this: to believe in the one whom he has sent" (John 6:29 NIV). Satan says, "No, your good life will satisfy God." And all who believe that lie become a part of Satan's rebellion.

Article 2

Demons also teach that Jesus is not what He claimed to be: the most unique person in all the universe. He claimed to be God Himself, while obviously at the same time he was a man. God and man in the same person. That's unique.

Satan and his demons attack both aspects of Jesus' person. They sometimes flatly deny that Jesus is God. At other times they try to make people think He was some kind of ghostlike appearance, not actually a human being.

Both errors have been around for a long time. In the first century there were demon-inspired preachers who said that Jesus was not actually a human being but merely an appearance of God in human form (1 John 4:2, 3). But what difference does that make? We would still know His teachings and have the example of His life, even if He were not an actual man. Yes, but then He would not have been able to die. Ghosts and apparitions don't die. God doesn't die, and if Jesus were only an appearance of God in the form of a human being, He could not have died. And if he did not die, then He did not pay the penalty for man's sins. Pseudosaviors do not have to die for their followers, but the true Savior did. And to do that, He had to be a human being.

But it wasn't enough for just any man to die. Only if God were involved could there be a satisfactory payment for the penalty of sin. So Jesus, to be a sufficient Savior, had to be God. And that's exactly what He claimed to be.

The Proof Is in the Walking

Do you remember the story of the paralyzed man whose friends let him down through a hole in the roof in order that Jesus might heal him? When Jesus saw the poor man He said, "Son, your sins are forgiven" (Mark 2:5 NIV). But some of the Jewish religious leaders, horrified at what He said, accused Jesus of blasphemy of the worst kind. He had made Himself equal with God by that statement. How so? Only God can forgive sins, the Jewish leaders well knew; so when Jesus declared the sick man's sins forgiven, He claimed to be God. Then Jesus posed a question: "Which is easier: to say to the paralytic, 'Your sins are forgiven,' or to say, 'Get up, take your mat and walk'?" (Mark 2:9 NIV). The answer is obvious. It is much easier to *say,* "Your sins be forgiven." Who can test the validity of such a statement? Where is the empirical proof that they have been forgiven? But if Jesus said, "Rise and walk," the empirical proof is evident to all. If the paralyzed man gets up, Jesus is God; if he doesn't, Jesus is a fake, an impostor, and a liar.

> He got up, took his mat and walked out in full view of them all. . . .
>
> Mark 2:12 NIV

The Truth, the Whole Truth, and Nothing but the Truth

Later, Jesus stood before Caiaphas, the high priest of Judaism. His very life was on the line. Caiaphas placed Him under oath and asked

Him if he claimed to be Israel's Messiah, God Himself. Listen to Jesus' reply: He said, "Yes, it is as you say" (Matthew 26:64 NIV). Look at Caiaphas' reaction: "Then the high priest tore his clothes and said, 'He has spoken blasphemy!' " (Matthew 26:65 NIV). Jesus staked His life on the truth that He is God, and He paid for His claim with His life.

No God-man, no true Savior. Satan knows this, so he concentrates his attack against that truth.

Demons are busy today promoting heresies about Christ, and they will step up their activities as the end nears. There is no need for salvation, they teach, and even if there were, you could not find it in Jesus Christ. In that coming time of trouble, this teaching will be even more intensified. In spite of all that men will experience during those terrible days, they will not turn in repentance to the true Savior.

Keeping Body and Soul Together

Remember the locusts in Revelation 9:1–11 (chapter 4)? Demon-locusts from the pit, led by a mighty angel called the Destroyer, will torment people with their scorpionlike stings for five months. Satan knows the fine art of adapting his techniques in order to achieve his ends. In the latter part of that seven-year time of trouble some men will refuse to bow down and worship him. In his anger, Satan will send a horde of demons to afflict the people. By tormenting their bodies, he hopes to capture their souls.

And he will be successful. Listen to how that ninth chapter closes: ". . . they did not stop worshiping demons, and idols of gold, silver, bronze, stone and wood—idols that cannot see or hear or walk. Nor did they repent of their murders, their magic arts, their sexual immorality or their thefts" (Revelation 9:20, 21 NIV). In that coming day men will actually worship demons.

Is that so far out? Look around. Remember, there are ten thousand professional astrologers in America today; ten million Americans are addicted to astrology and as many as forty million dabble in it. Statistics about the organized Church of Satan are hard to obtain, but the number of members has been estimated to be as high as ten thousand . . . and that's in the headquarters city of San Francisco alone! Spiritist churches claim to meet in six thousand different locations each week. And this is just the beginning; more demon worship is on the way.

Dr. Satan, M.D.

Satan has not only a Ph.D. in religion but also an M.D. He practices sorcery! The word *sorcery* means to practice magic, mix poisons, or prepare magic potions. Satan will attack people's bodies in an attempt to destroy them. Undoubtedly he will have plenty of help from people themselves; he won't need to personally supervise each case! People will want to poison themselves with drugs in order to numb the effects of the trouble they find themselves in. Others will poison themselves as part of their worship of demons. Demons and drugs will be wedded in those coming tribulation days. The religion of demons and the life of drugs—that's the awesome outlook.

An Up-to-Date Warning

What does the Lord God think of Dr. Satan and his medical practice? Listen to what He said thirty-four hundred years ago:

> Don't let anyone live who practices black magic, or witchcraft, or who interprets omens, or a sorcerer, or one who casts a spell, or a medium, or a spiritist, or who calls up the spirits of the dead. Anyone doing these things is detestable to the Lord.
>
> Deuteronomy 18:10–12

The Final Act

Let's review the military campaigns of the tribulation days. Antichrist, as ruler of a western federation, will bring three of the ten nations into his alliance by force. Egypt and Russia will launch a pincer attack against Israel. Antichrist will come to Israel's defense, defeating Egypt and temporarily holding back Russia. While Antichrist and his forces are in the south, Russia (the King of the North) will amass additional troops in Israel, but God will destroy them. When Antichrist returns to Israel he will find the hordes of people from the north . . . all dead. This will leave him with only one enemy, the Kings of the East. As these two great foes prepare to meet in the land of Palestine, Jesus Christ will return and conquer them all in the climactic final act of world history called Armageddon.

Battle or War?

We have grown accustomed to thinking of the Battle of Armageddon as if it were a single engagement in one location. This is not true. The Bible describes a war or campaign (Revelation 16:14), and Armageddon is only one of its focal points. Technically it should be called the War of the Great Day of God Almighty. Several battles and much geography will be involved, though the action will center in Palestine.

A Historic Hill

Armageddon means the mountain of Megiddo. Strategically located about twenty miles south-southeast of the modern city Haifa, the valley of Megiddo has been the scene of many battles. The ancient fortress city of Megiddo stands on the southwest edge of the Esdraelon plain adjacent to the Carmel ridge at the intersection of the main north-south pass on the route between Mesopotamia and Egypt. This strategic position made the city an important trade and military center. Today the valley covers an area of twenty miles by fourteen miles. By the end of the tribulation days that area will be reduced considerably because of the earthquakes and other catastrophes that will affect the topography.

As long ago as 1468 B.C. we have a record of Thutmose III defeating the Canaanites at Armageddon. When the Israelites conquered Palestine under General Joshua they were unable to occupy Megiddo, so the Canaanites continued to rule the area. King Josiah was killed there. Mighty King Solomon rebuilt the city of Megiddo and fortified it (1 Kings 9:15). Ruins are still visible of the stables he built for his horses and chariots, the cistern dug to provide water for the animals, the pillars punched with holes for hitching them, and the spacious area that accommodated 450 horses.

Today the lush valley of Megiddo, rich and beautiful, is called the Breadbasket of Israel. Someday it will turn into the Bloodbath of Israel, a scene of death and desolation.

Jerusalem, Too

Israel is a country of short distances. Mountains and plains, city and village, fertile fields and deserts are often minutes apart. Israel can be crossed by car in ninety minutes. Only fifty miles separate Jerusalem and Armageddon, but that last war will combine them into a single enormous battlefield. Listen to what the prophet Zechariah wrote twenty-four hundred years ago:

> For I will gather all the nations against Jerusalem to battle, and the city will be captured, the houses plundered, the women

ravished, and half of the city exiled, but the rest of the people will not be cut off from the city.

Zechariah 14:2 NAS

When will these things take place? Just prior to the Lord's coming, when "His feet will stand on the Mount of Olives" (Zechariah 14:4 NAS). So Armageddon will not be confined to Megiddo. It will spill over into all of Israel, raging even into Jerusalem.

A River of Blood

All the battles + All the land = A bloodbath. John saw it, and described it this way: "They were trampled in the winepress outside the city, and blood flowed out of the press, rising as high as the horse's bridles for a distance of 1,600 stadia [about 200 miles]" (Revelation 14:20 NIV).

A winepress makes a vivid illustration of Armageddon. It consisted of two receptacles, or vats, placed at different levels. In the upper one the grapes were stamped out, while the lower one received the juice. In this last war, men's lives will be stamped out, and the blood will surge through the land like a mighty river two hundred miles in length and about four and one-half feet deep.

Can this really be true? Remember, Armageddon will not be a single battle but a continuous war starting with the King of the South, the King of the North, and Antichrist clashing head-on in Israel. It will continue with the slaughter of the Russian hordes on the mountains of Israel, and will climax with the confrontation between East and West in Megiddo. Such a river of blood, though it stretches the imagination, is not at all impossible.

Satan, Chairman of the Board

Genius generals, proud politicians, and scheming Satan—they will all have their places in the Armageddon Army.

The generals will plan the battle strategy. The politicians will plot the nations' involvement. But the Prince of Darkness will be Chairman of the Board and Chief Executive Officer.

The apostle John in his vision saw three powerful demons going to the kings of the world to gather them to the War of the Great Day of God Almighty. One of the demons comes directly from Satan, another from Antichrist, and the third from Antichrist's prime minister (Revelation 16:13, 14). Here will be Satan's Last Stand, his final attempt to deceive the nations into thinking they can succeed in rebelling against God. And he will muster his troops, the demons, in this final do-or-die effort.

For the Birds

But death will exact a terrible toll, and the men will fall everywhere. By the thousands. By the millions. The Bible describes the scene with vivid eloquence.

> I saw heaven standing open and there before me was a white horse, whose rider is called Faithful and True. With justice he judges and makes war. . . . The armies of heaven were following him, riding on white horses. . . . Out of his mouth comes a sharp sword with which to strike down the nations. . . . On his robe and on his thigh he has this name written: KING OF KINGS AND LORD OF LORDS.
>
> Revelation 19:11–16 NIV

The carnage will be staggering. Generals, sergeants, privates, and captains; merchants, politicians, old women, and teenagers; horses and more horses will all die in battle. So the Creator will order the birds in the sky to help clean up all those dead bodies.

". . . and all the birds gorged themselves on their flesh" (Revelation 19:21 NIV).

The Living End

What about Satan and his board of directors? Satan, defeated at last, will be bound in the abyss so that he can deceive the nations of the world no longer. Antichrist and his prime minister will be "thrown alive into the fiery lake of burning sulfur" (Revelation 19:20 NIV). But notice carefully, their capture is not the end, for they will still be living in their places of torment.

A Personal Plea

You have read in this chapter what God and His prophets have said about the power of the devil. Everyone is free to accept or reject what he has learned. But these voices are saying something that ought to be heeded. The power of the occult is growing, wrapping its tentacles around many individuals and sectors of society. That power will increase until it squeezes men to death at Armageddon. But for all the power that Satan has, he cannot defeat Jesus Christ. His doom is certain, and so is that of his fellow rebels.

The plea of this chapter is simply this: Don't dabble in the occult. You may be exposing yourself to forces that you cannot control. That's exactly what will happen on a worldwide scale in those future days of trouble. Men will be in league with Satan and will be unable to stop their own destruction.

But it can happen now to individuals. One of Satan's greatest deceptions is to make us think it can happen only to the other fellow. But that's exactly what the other fellow believes too. How can you defend yourself against such a powerful enemy? The only sure course of action is to open yourself to the power of the living Christ. He alone is greater than Satan.

10
No Tricentennial for the U.S.A.

> Your Republic will be fearfully plundered and laid waste by
> barbarians in the 20th century as the Roman Empire was in
> the 5th century, with this difference—the Huns and Vandals
> who ravaged the Roman Empire came from without, and your
> Huns and Vandals will have been engendered within your own
> country, by your own institutions.

So predicted British historian Thomas Macaulay more than 125 years
ago.

Nations rise and nations fall. It's a two-way street.

The might of ancient Babylon lasted only 86 years.

The powerful Persian Empire did better—208 years.

The glory of Greece was eclipsed after 268 years.

Mighty Rome ruled for almost 9 centuries.

The British Empire endured for about 250 years.

The United States of America is now celebrating her bicentennial.
If we make it to a tricentennial, we will beat the averages.

Now the fourth-largest country in the world, both in area and
population, the United States was largely a wilderness three hundred
years ago. But thousands came from many lands and varied back-
grounds to forge a nation that has blessed its people with the highest
standard of living in the world. Rich in natural resources, technology,
educational opportunities, and culture, our country seems invincible.
Yet the great oil embargo of 1974 disrupted many areas of life and
demonstrated our nation's vulnerability. Military experts warn that
other nations are capable of destroying our major cities at the push
of a button. No longer does the United States excel in all phases of
military power. What lies ahead for this great country?

All Nations Under God

The Pledge of Allegiance to the flag boldly declares that the United
States is "one nation under God." Every nation in the world could

truthfully write this phrase into its pledge, for all nations are under God. Many do not realize it, but the fact remains.

The Brilliance of Babylon

King Nebuchadnezzar said: "Is not this great Babylon, which I have built for the royal dwelling-place by the might of my power and for the glory of my majesty?" (Daniel 4:30). And he was right. Nebuchadnezzar stands as one of antiquity's greatest men for his role in creating the worldwide glory of Babylon six centuries before Christ. Though brilliant and daring, a man of force and decision, the great king had to learn one lesson the hard way.

The Crazy King

At the zenith of his power, King Nebuchadnezzar went insane. He needed to learn an important lesson from the King of kings. He needed to realize that "the Most High is ruler over the realm of mankind, and bestows it on whomever he wishes" (Daniel 4:25 NAS). That's a difficult lesson for any ruler or nation to learn; in Nebuchadnezzar's case, God had to humble him to the place of insanity in order to drive home the point.

The king was a dreamer. In addition to his dream about a great image (chapter 3) he had another alarming dream about the future, as related to us in chapter 4 of the Book of Daniel.

The king was also a slow learner. When he dreamed about the great statue, we saw earlier, he called upon the magicians and sorcerers, the wise men of his kingdom, to recount and interpret his dream, and they could not. Oh, they could "dream up" an interpretation, but they could not dream up the dream. Finally Daniel was brought before the king and told him the contents of the dream and what it meant.

One would think that after such an experience, Nebuchadnezzar would know the true prophets from the fakes. But he didn't. So when a second dream perplexed the king, he duplicated his error. He called for the fakers again. Naturally, they couldn't tell him the interpretation of his dream, so Daniel, the true prophet, was summoned.

Daniel found himself with the unpleasant task of telling the king, whom he had obviously grown to respect and love, that he was going to go crazy for seven years. During the king's illness he would imagine himself as a wild animal and, at least at times, he would act like one. A year later it happened exactly as the prophet predicted.

Nebuchadnezzar was seized by lycanthropy. Or, more accurately, boanthropy (that's when a man assumes he is an ox; lycanthropy, when he thinks he is a wolf). For seven years the king was secluded in the royal woods where he could be cared for and where the secret of his insanity could be carefully concealed from his unsuspecting subjects.

When his sanity at last returned, he had learned his lesson. Listen to what the mighty king wrote:

> I blessed the Most High and praised and honored Him who lives forever;
>
> > For His dominion is an everlasting dominion,
> > And His kingdom endures from generation to generation.
> > "And all the inhabitants of the earth are accounted as nothing,
> > But He does according to His will in the host of heaven
> > And among the inhabitants of earth;
> > And no one can ward off His hand
> > Or say to Him, 'What hast Thou done?' "
>
> Daniel 4:34, 35 NAS

A hard lesson, yes, and a hard way to learn it. But how terribly important!

Paul Pounds Home the Point

Six hundred years later some other important people were reminded of the same truth. The apostle Paul had arrived in Athens on his second missionary journey. Facing the Epicurean and Stoic philosophers of that day, he reminded them that the God of heaven determines when nations will prosper, and exactly how far their kingdoms will extend (Acts 17:26). Imagine Paul boldly flinging such a statement into the faces of those who were citizens of mighty Rome. Imagine him preaching like that to affluent Americans or thriving Third World nations today, telling them that God has already determined the limits of their expansion, the extent of their influence, and the duration of their importance in world affairs.

The Clouded Crystal Ball

The Bible has made crystal clear the destiny of many nations. Babylon, Persia, Greece, Rome, Egypt, Russia, and Israel can read their futures today in the pages of Scripture as certainly as if they were reading history. But not so with the United States and many other nations such as Canada, Australia, and the countries of Latin America. In these cases the Bible is silent. Yet even its comparative silence says something.

The Sounds of Silence

The Bible's silence concerning the future of the United States might well mean that she will play no prominent role in the end-time drama. A nation does not have to be named in order to be identified in Bible prophecy. When Ezekiel described the future Russian invasion he used the phrase "remote parts of the north" (38:15 NAS). Surely some prophet would have predicted something about those countries or peoples in the remote parts of the west if God had intended a major end-time role for them in the western hemisphere. The fact is that no one did.

So the silence may be telling us that (1) either the United States will be subordinated to a relatively unimportant role in world affairs, or (2) the United States will be wiped out by nuclear war or natural catastrophe prior to the end time.

The Balance of Power

High priority in the study and management of foreign affairs goes to the concept of "balance of power." As I write, an admiral of the U.S. Navy is pleading for no additional cuts in military spending because of the increased strength of the Russian navy. Several nations are struggling to maintain the delicate balance of power in the Middle East. The members of the Nuclear Club watch each other warily for any new test that might signal the slightest imbalance of power.

The Bible describes clearly the power blocs which will exist during those coming years of great trial on earth. The first two to clash will be the bloc in the west (headed by Antichrist) and the northern power (led by Russia). When the northern army is annihilated, the Kings of the East will jump into the fray, and at Armageddon East will meet West.

Is there room in this picture for a large power bloc in the western hemisphere headed by the United States? It seems unlikely, for that would pose too great a threat to the others. Instead, we are led to conclude that the United States will be neutralized, subordinated, or wiped out, thus having little or no part in the political and military affairs of the end time.

A Hint From our Heritage

It is not too farfetched to envision the United States someday aligned with the Western Confederation of Nations which will be formed by Antichrist. National origin could be the link, since many U.S. citizens originally came from the countries which will make up that Western alliance of nations.

The United States has received a larger number of immigrants than any other country in history. The thirteen original states were settled mostly by colonists from the British Isles. In 1780 more than three-fourths of the American population were descendants from English and Irish settlers. The rest came from Germany, the Netherlands, France, and Switzerland.

Between 1841 and 1860 over four million newcomers found homes in the United States. Almost all came from Ireland, Germany, Great Britain, and France. In 1882 three out of every four immigrants came from northern and western Europe. By 1896 more than half the immigrants originated from countries in southern and eastern Europe, such as Italy and Austria-Hungary.

So when the European Federation of Nations rises to power, the United States may find herself in a supportive role in favor of this powerful alliance and in opposition to the other power blocs in Russia, Africa, and the Far East. This would mean that the United States, haven of Christianity for two centuries, will find herself in league with Antichrist.

None of these options—third-rate power, desolated wasteland, or backer of Antichrist—paints a very bright future for the United States.

The Great Society

What makes a nation great? Economic power? Military might? The answer obviously depends on the standard by which greatness is measured. If God delights in goodness, generosity, and justice, then the nation that practices these will be great in God's estimation.

But there's more to greatness than these things. God has two other exceedingly important interests. One is the Jewish people; the other, the world.

How to Be a Friend of God

High praise is paid to the patriarch Abraham when he is called "the friend of God" (2 Chronicles 20:7; Isaiah 41:8; James 2:23). The

Jewish people, descendants of Abraham through Isaac and Jacob, are the apple of God's eye (Zechariah 2:8). Observe the closeness of the relationship between God and Abraham, between Abraham and his descendants, and between God and the Jewish people. It is small wonder that God solemnly declared to Abraham: "I will bless those who bless you, and the one who curses you I will curse" (Genesis 12:3 NAS). The friends and enemies of Abraham and his progeny are the friends and enemies of God.

History has verified this principle. Blessing has often been the lot of individuals and nations who have treated Abraham and the Jewish people kindly. On the other hand, anti-Semitism has been punished by some kind of judgment from God. As we have seen, God is not through with the Jewish people, and therefore He carefully watches to see how individuals and nations treat them today.

So far the United States has received good marks on God's report card in dealing with the Jews. Abraham's descendants have fared well in America. Anti-Semitism has never been strong. The United States was one of the first countries to recognize the State of Israel in 1948. Much of the money needed to sustain that state has come from the U.S. government or from prosperous American Jews.

This does not mean, however, that the United States must condone every action taken by the State of Israel. People, not politics, are God's chief concern; and the Jewish people, not Israeli politics, should be the Christian's interest.

But what of the future? After the true Church is removed from this earth (chapter 12), what will be America's attitude toward the Jewish people? With no Christian citizens to protest injustices, it is not inconceivable that anti-Semitism and persecution will break out in the United States, bringing God's judgment on America.

In the meanwhile let America remember that a great nation is marked by her kind treatment of the Jewish people. God keeps His promises and He will bless those who are friendly toward the "friend of God" and his descendants.

Beautiful People

But God is also vitally interested in all the other people of the world. That's precisely why He sent His only Son, Jesus Christ, to this planet. By His death He made it possible for all men everywhere to become friends of God. But people must convey that message to the world. And those who do are called beautiful people (Romans

10:15)! So again it is not inconceivable that God has been merciful to the United States simply because so many people have financed and personally taken the good news of the Gospel to others in this world. A Church that loses its concern for missions at home and abroad, or a Congress that discourages charitable giving, runs a risk of incurring God's disfavor.

What does this all mean? Simply this: There are no definite prophecies concerning the United States in the Bible, but there are some logical options. She will be wiped out, neutralized as a third-rate power, or aligned with Antichrist and the Western Federation of Nations. In the meantime she should never forget two important lessons: Be good to the Jewish people, for this pleases God; and be concerned with the spread of the Gospel of God's salvation to the whole world, for this is in accord with God's program for today.

11

Superchurch

Religion is big business today. Admittedly, the polls tell us that not as many people are attending church as in the past, but church is only one small part of religion.

Many church memberships are mushrooming. A recent book entitled *Why Conservative Churches Are Growing* probes the subject of explosive church growth. In some countries of the world, Pentecostalism represents the fastest-growing church group in history. Revival sweeps the churches of Indonesia. The charismatic movement attracts thousands who were formerly indifferent to religion.

Surrounding Christianity in its various forms are numerous other religions which attract their share of followers. Zealous devotees of Hare Krishna with shaved heads, draped clothing, and beads are a common sight on the streets of many cities. Aspects of the occult are highly commercialized. For a fee you can feed your birthdate into a computer. Then at any future time, for only the price of a phone call to the computer headquarters, you can have your daily horoscope read to you. Many newspapers also carry the daily horoscope. Witches and warlocks have invaded the bumper-sticker market. Even the sacred cow of science is being pushed around by those who demand explanations and answers that science is unable to give.

The mergers of several denominations in recent years has been a remarkable phenomenon. Groups that once were fiercely independent have joined forces. Efforts to further the trend today have met with increasing resistance, but the push toward church unification continues. What does the future hold for the Church?

What Church?
The label "church" is stuck on almost anything today. Mainline churches are so designated. But storefront groups are also dubbed churches. Pseudoscientific organizations are labeled churches. Even Satan has his churches. Obviously, we need to define our terms carefully.

Jesus Christ's Church is the one true Church. You see, the word *church* means "belonging to the Lord." Later, it came to mean any religious group, but in the strict sense of the word it means "the group that belongs to the Lord." They are the ones who make up the true Church.

Of course, many belong to institutions called churches who do not belong to the Lord Jesus Christ. But only those who through faith have received Him as their Savior actually comprise the real Church, the one that God calls His own.

A Disappearing Act

Just before that unique seven-year period of trouble begins, God is going to do something spectacular with His true Church. He is going to remove it from the earth. That's right—every believer in Christ will disappear from the earth. Naturally, none of these people will experience the horrible judgments that are coming.

The apostle Paul described the event this way: "For the Lord Himself will descend from heaven with a shout, with the voice of the archangel, and with the trumpet of God; and the dead in Christ shall rise first. Then we who are alive and remain shall be caught up together with them in the clouds to meet the Lord in the air . . ." (1 Thessalonians 4:16, 17 NAS).

Fantastic? Perhaps. But think how many other things which you now accept as commonplace were fantastic when they first appeared on the scene. The telephone. The airplane. Men on the moon. Computers. Television. Rockets to Mars. This great disappearing act will happen only once. But happen it will.

Can you imagine the scene if this event should occur some Sunday morning about 11:55? Many people will be attending church. Some will belong to the Lord; some will only belong to the church. Some of the choir will be true believers in Christ; some will not. Now the drama begins. The service is about to close. Suddenly and without warning, some of the congregation immediately disappear into thin air. A few of the choir vanish. Some of the ushers disappear from their posts. Maybe the preacher vanishes. Maybe not. The service breaks up in chaos. People run for home and for their TVs, where they hear commentators excitedly reporting the mysterious disappearance of people here and there. Some cities have been widely affected. Others have scarcely noticed anything amiss. Those people who are left behind want some fast answers. News will be tightly regulated, and carefully worded answers will eventually be given. When the initial panic dies down, people will resume their normal course of living. But the nagging question will remain: What happened? Where did they go? Why am I left?

Maybe some will remember that they heard a preacher talk about this once. Maybe some will even open a Bible to 1 Thessalonians 4:13 or 1 Corinthians 15:51 and see how it was all predicted to take place just the way it happened. Though they will have missed the rapture personally, it will still not be too late to seek God's forgiveness through Jesus Christ.

Carry On, O Church

At that moment there will not be a single true Christian on the entire earth. But there will be plenty of religious people, and they will have their heyday. A great religious organization will flourish during the first half of that unique seven-year period of trouble that is coming. To call this organization a church would be far too flattering, since it in no way belongs to the Lord. "False church" would be closer to the truth.

Introducing . . . Babylon the Great!

Its name will be Babylon the Great (Revelation 17:5). To be sure, individual congregations will use some other names over the doors of their churches, but God calls this false church Babylon the Great. Why? Because the name fits the character.

Babylon comes from a word that means confusion, or mixing. Babylon the Great will be the ultimate in organized confusion. Babylon began way back with the Tower of Babel (Genesis 11:9). You may remember that those who built the Tower of Babel intended the building to become the symbol of God-defying disobedience and pride. Under Hammurabi and Nebuchadnezzar, Babylon reached great prominence in the world. But in the New Testament, ancient Babylon is referred to as the archetypal head of all entrenched worldly resistance to God. Babylon is the fountainhead of all earthly rebellion against God. Babylon is more than a city; it is an organized anti-God system.

What do we mean when we talk of Wall Street? Only a street in lower Manhattan? No, we are referring to the whole financial system which does business on Wall Street. When the news commentator says, "Wall Street interpreted the rally as . . ." he means that brokers across the nation (not merely on Wall Street) made the interpretation. *The Wall Street Journal* gives news of financial transactions on Wall Street—and also of those occurring in Chicago, London, Tokyo, and a host of other places. Thus, Wall Street is both a location and a system. Likewise, the Babylonian "Church" will meet in specific locations, but the term represents all organized opposition to God and the kingdom of Christ.

Cherchez la Femme

In chapter 17 of the Book of Revelation, we have a remarkable picture of the *religious system,* Babylon. Remarkable because it is so detailed. Remarkable because it dovetails with other prophecies we have already discussed. Remarkable because it will come true.

Babylon the Great is portrayed in the drama of this chapter as a woman. Not an ordinary woman, but a harlot. Quite obviously, she is a church that is unfaithful to Christ. Indeed, four times in the chapter she is called a harlot. As a harlot she prostitutes everything for her own self-aggrandizement. Furthermore she is not just an ordinary harlot, she is the *great* harlot (verse 1). She represents the epitome of unfaithfulness.

Second, look where she is sitting: "on many waters"—a symbolic phrase that would be difficult for us to interpret, were it not explained in the verses following. The many waters where the harlot sits "are peoples and multitudes and nations and tongues" (verse 15 NAS). Babylon the Great will be great in its extent, stretching around the world. The technical term for this is *ecumenical,* a word derived from the Greek and meaning "the inhabited world." Since this organization will include many peoples and nations, it can properly be called ecumenical.

Third, Babylon will be politically powerful. Enter Antichrist again, only this time he doesn't look so powerful, for the harlot church is actually sitting on him! The symbolism is clear: For a while, at least, Babylon will be able to manipulate Antichrist. This won't last long, as we shall see. But during the early years of that seven-year period, the false church will exercise great political clout through Antichrist.

How can this be? Why would a powerful alliance of nations, such as the Western alliance, need to hide behind the skirts of a harlot religious system? Perhaps the threat of godless communism and other ideologies will force the move. People may think they need a religious defense against atheism, and in the process will rush into the arms of the harlot church.

Fourth, Babylon the Great will be luxuriously enticing. Inwardly she is a slut; outwardly she is stylish—"clothed in purple and scarlet, and adorned with gold and precious stones and pearls . . ." (Revelation 17:4 NAS). All of this outward splendor is only a cover-up for her sinister purpose of leading her followers into idolatry.

Fifth, the particular organizational form this great religious system will take appears to be a federation. She herself is called a harlot, but she is also called the mother of harlots. Perhaps her "family" will include various religions, all of them unfaithful to the Lord and together comprising this great Superchurch.

Of course, a federation will be much easier to organize than a union. Unions involve individual groups giving up their identities and distinctive practices; in a federation, particular religions can keep their distinctions and yet join together in this "family" relationship.

Sixth, she will persecute to the death those who are true followers of the Lord during this time. She will be drunk with their blood. She will hound them to death. She will be totally intolerant of opposition.

But who will be around to oppose her? Didn't we say that all true believers will have disappeared from the earth just before Babylon the Great appears? Yes, but new believers will arise, risking their very lives in their decision to follow Christ. Of course, they will speak out against the idolatry and unfaithfulness and wickedness of Babylon the Great, and many will die for their convictions.

Turning the Tables

Superchurch is doomed. The structure so carefully built will one day come crashing down. For three and one-half years nothing will block the religious and political plans of Superchurch. But as suddenly as she gained her power, she will lose it. And to make matters worse, her defeat will come at the hands of her ally, the Western Federation of Nations. The ten-nation federation under her sway will suddenly turn on her and destroy her completely.

Then there will be no more church, not even a false one. Do you see how this all fits together? Antichrist, the head of that ten-nation federation, wants to be worshiped himself. Obviously this is not possible as long as Superchurch is competing for the honor. So either Antichrist must abandon his plans, or he must destroy Superchurch. He chooses the latter course. Now the way is clear for him to stand in the Holy Place of the temple in Jerusalem and demand to be worshiped. No more of the beautiful idolatry promoted by Superchurch. In its place, the crassest form of idolatry, the worship of a man or his image, will be substituted.

All Roads Lead to Superchurch

The year 1894 marked the beginning of the Christian ecumenical movement with the organization of the Open Church League. In 1900 it became the National Federation of Churches and Christian Workers. In 1905 this was replaced by the Federal Council of Churches of Christ in America. The name was changed again in 1950 to the National Council of Churches of Christ in the U.S.A. The stated purpose of the Federal Council was to bring together all who called themselves Christian. Its only doctrinal basis was stated in the preamble which recognized Jesus as "divine Lord and Savior." But nothing was said about His being the *only* divine Lord and Savior.

Superchurch hit a milestone in 1948. In that year the World Council of Churches was formed in Amsterdam, composed of delegates from 135 denominational bodies. Today it represents a constituency of 315 million and is second only to the Roman Catholic Church in size and influence. In 1961 another milestone was reached when the W.C.C. received into membership the Russian Orthodox Church.

Though the Roman Catholic Church does not hold membership in the World Council, cooperation and talks between the two groups continue. The fourth assembly of the Council, held in Uppsala, Sweden in 1968, went on record as encouraging "the Joint Working Group to continue to give attention to the question of the membership of the Roman Catholic Church in the World Council of Churches. . . . The World Council reaffirms its eagerness to extend its membership to include all those Christian Churches at present outside its fellowship."

At that same assembly Father Roberto Tucci stated that "Roman Catholic ecclesiology did not make membership [in the W.C.C.] impossible." The assembly affirmed that "from the side of the World Council of Churches there was in principle, no obstacle to the membership of the Roman Catholic Church in the Council."

Another Ecumenical Baby

The year 1962 saw the birth of another ecumenical movement in the United States. The Consultation on Church Union (known as

COCU) was fathered by Eugene Carson Blake, then Stated Clerk of the United Presbyterian Church in the U.S.A. It was an attempt to unite Dr. Blake's group, the Protestant Episcopal Church, the Methodist Church, and the United Church of Christ. Other groups joined the discussions. In 1968 the Methodist Church merged with the Evangelical United Brethren Church to form the United Methodist Church.

Both groups, the National Council of Churches and COCU, are experiencing hard times in the 1970s. Money is scarce; budgets aren't being met; church union is no longer the "in" thing. In 1973 the Presbyterian Church (U.S.A.) withdrew from COCU. But COCU is still far from dead. And its main interest continues to be the achievement of cooperation with groups still outside the fold, in an attempt to woo them into membership. Late in 1974 COCU's chief executive said that a very important part of his job was to "develop, cultivate and maintain relationships" with evangelicals and others not in COCU.

In 1974 the U.S. executive secretary in the World Council admitted that "people are asking, as never before, Is ecumenism out of date?" (*Eternity,* January 1975). At the same time, Pope Paul VI was addressing a meeting of 207 prelates gathered in Rome to discuss the future of the Roman Catholic Church. "The Church," he stated, "is in difficulty . . . [and] seems destined to die" (*Sunday Magazine,* December 8, 1974).

What Next?

Discussions have been pointing for some time to the eventual establishment of a new organization to replace the N.C.C. and the W.C.C. For example, in December 1969 the General Secretary of the N.C.C., R. H. Edwin Espy, called for the creation of a "more representative" body. He said the "new 'General Ecumenical Council' could function as an organizational umbrella for a large variety of interdenominational agencies . . . [embracing] Roman Catholics, Pentecostals, and other Christians who are not now among its 33 Protestant and Orthodox member churches" (*Newsweek,* December 15, 1969, p. 97).

Organizations may come and go, but the march toward church union goes steadily forward.

Money Talks

Though cash may be scarce, the churches' assets are enormous. At the beginning of this decade the visible assets (land and buildings) of the churches in the United States totaled at least $80 billion, almost double the combined assets of the nation's five largest industrial corporations. Of this total, about $45 billion was held by Roman Catholics, $28 billion by Protestants, and $7 billion by the Jewish faith. Denominational pension funds, mortgages, and annuities now total more than $2 billion. Churches not only invest in businesses but even own some outright. This led Eugene Carson Blake, during his tenure as General Secretary of the World Council of Churches, to warn: "When one remembers that churches pay no inheritance taxes (churches do not die); that churches may own and operate business and be exempt from the 52 per cent corporate income tax, and that real property used for church purposes (which in some states are most generously construed) is tax exempt, it is not unreasonable to prophesy that with reasonably prudent management, the churches ought to be able to control the whole economy of the nation within the predictable future." And this prediction comes from someone within the movement!

> And the woman was clothed in purple and scarlet, and adorned with gold and precious stones and pearls. . . .
>
> Revelation 17:4 NAS

The Doctrinal Road to Unity

Even a false church has to have some kind of doctrinal basis. What sort of doctrine could ever satisfy all the variety of groups that will eventually form Babylon the Great?

There are at least two theologies in full bloom today that could very well fill the bill. One is universalism; the other is the Theology of Hope.

Universalism is not new. It has been around since the second century after Christ, and it teaches that ultimately all men will be saved and go to heaven. Other tenets of universalism include unitarianism (God exists in only one person, Himself; there is no Trinity), the varied character of divine revelation (in contrast to ultimate revelation in the Bible), the humanness of Christ, and a denial of His deity. The first universalist congregation in America was formed in 1779. In 1942 the group welcomed all humane men, whether Christian or not, into its fellowship. In May 1961 there was a merger with the Unitarian church to form the Unitarian-Universalist Association.

With doctrines like that, you need no conversions. Everybody can find a comfortable place under the umbrella. The mission of the

church is to inform people that all is well, not to convert them to a
Person or a belief. The universalist proclaims that the light is on in
the room: Open your eyes and see it. If you do, fine; if you don't, fine.
Eventually everyone will see the light. Biblical Christianity says that
Jesus Christ is the only Light of the world. To see Him, you must
have new eyes, for all are blinded by sin and incapable of seeing apart
from faith in Him.

Universalism is not confined to the Unitarian-Universalist Association. Much liberal theology includes the belief in ultimate salvation
for all. Some who may be called neoorthodox or Barthian also em-
brace this teaching. Even some conservatives (in Germany, for example) hold a universal viewpoint. Universalism enjoys wide acceptance,
and could easily be embraced by a Superchurch.

Hope and Revolution

But what of the second possible Superchurch platform? In Europe
it is called the Theology of Hope. In Latin America it is called the
Theology of Revolution. Though there are apparently no organizational links, these theologies are saying nearly the same thing.

The scenario goes like this: When we look at the past, all we see
is chaos in society. What we expect in the future is utopia. The job
of the present is to change chaos to utopia. Anything that gets the
job done is legitimate, including violent overthrow of governments,
if that be necessary. And all of this takes place in the name of religion.

The leading exponent of this theology in Europe is Jurgen Molt-
mann of Tubingen, Germany. His goal is a universal church totally
involved with the world community. He says: "Only by means of a
universal church can the world attain a universal government"
(*Schwäbisches Tagblatt* vom 22.2.1973).

This spirit of anarchy is also supported by the Theology of Revolution in Latin America. The chief task, if not the sole task, of the
church is to promote social justice by any and all means. Existing
social structures oppress the masses and must be overthrown if true
liberation is to be known. Salvation, according to these theologians,
consists in liberating people from socioeconomic and sociopolitical
oppression in the world. (*See* Gustave Gutiérrez, *A Theology of Liberation.*)

At the All Africa Conference of Churches in Zambia in 1974 the
same theme was heard (as reported by Byang H. Kato, *Perception,*
published in Nairobi, Kenya, July 1974). The liberation movements

present there reworded the Lord's Prayer in terms of political liberation. Poems on liberation took the place of Bible reading. Violence
in support of liberation was paraded as the desirable goal of the
church. One speaker declared that "the goals of the church are the
goals of the State." Another flatly said: "Any outright rejection of
violence is an untenable alternative for African Christians. . . . In
accepting the violence of the Cross, God, in Jesus Christ, sanctified
violence into a redemptive instrument for bringing into being a fuller
human life." The revolutionary message comes through loud and
clear.

And I saw a woman sitting on a scarlet beast. . . .

Revelation 17:3 NAS

The Point

The Superchurch of World Religions is on its way: powerful, worldwide, and invincible—for three and one-half years.

The progress toward organizational unity waxes and wanes, but the
movement is steadily going forward. Whatever happens to ecumenical
organizations, however, don't overlook what is happening on the
theological scene. Universalism and revolution in the name of the
church are sweeping the theological world. Organizational unity and
theological heresy may be compared to two runners. One may pass
the other temporarily, causing the lead to seesaw back and forth
between them. But as they approach the finish line they will join
hands, and from their combined forces will emerge Superchurch.

The stage is set. The props are in place. The actors are in the wings.
The script has been written. Soon we'll hear, "Curtain!"

12

Moving Day for Wall Street

The Great Economic Upheaval of 1974 left the world in chaos. Quintupled prices for crude oil resulted in economic fallout that affected most of the industrial nations of the world.

The U.S. balance of payments deficit ballooned to $10.58 billion for all of 1974.

Saudi Arabia began to accumulate excess petrodollars at the rate of $20 billion a year.

The Shah of Iran announced plans to make his country the fifth-ranking industrial power in the world by 1990.

Shock waves rolled through the international banking community when King Faisal of Saudi Arabia was assassinated in April 1975. The Saudi government, possessor of the world's third-largest monetary reserves (after West Germany and the United States), was suddenly left for the moment in a state of limbo over who would manage its huge oil windfall dividends.

Overnight, economics has displaced ecology as the number one topic of conversation and concern. Sources of energy for our homes and cars have taken priority over concern for polluted rivers and skies. Politicians have been rudely awakened to the staggering ramifications of economics. Malcolm Muggeridge recently observed: "What is certain in sober truth is that the English are now threatened, in a matter of months rather than years, with the total disruption of their present way of life as never before in their history, not excepting either the Civil War in Cromwell's time or the occupation of the Channel ports by the Germans in 1940, and that on their response to this will depend their very survival as an independent sovereign nation" (*Esquire,* February 1975, p. 50).

Suddenly, economics has become the number one molding force in the world.

Take Another Bow, Babylon

Babylon, we saw in the last chapter, means confusion. It's the label God gives to the religious confusion of the ecumenical Superchurch.

But Babylon also stands for the confused economic system that is developing. Just as Wall Street stands for a specific location as well as a system of finance, so biblical Babylon names a particular place as well as a coming economic system.

Chapter 18 of the last book of the Bible describes this city and system. The detailed itemizing of merchants, merchandise, ships, sailors, and trade all add up to a description of a commercial system. Its destruction is also described—but more of that later.

What City?

But Babylon is also a city as well as a label for a system. The question is: What city? Only two serious candidates have ever been proposed.

One is Babylon. Formerly a great city on the Euphrates River but now deserted, Babylon is situated in the country of Iraq fifty-one miles south of modern Baghdad. The Bible ascribes the founding of the ancient city of Babylon to the followers of Nimrod (Genesis 10:8–10). About 1830 B.C. the city began its rise to prominence, reaching its pinnacle of glory under Nebuchadnezzar (605–562 B.C.). In 539 B.C. the Persians captured the city, though they spared the principal buildings. However, Xerxes destroyed Babylon in 478 B.C. and although there were attempts to restore it, the city fell into disrepair and ruins three hundred years before Christ.

Obviously if Babylon is to be the capital of world trade, it must first be rebuilt, and that appears to be an utter impossibility. But is it? Nothing seems impossible in these fast-moving days. As a matter of fact, the Associated Press reported on March 29, 1971 in a dispatch from Beirut that "Iraq announced a $30 million plan to rebuild according to its 'original architectural designs' the ancient city of Babylon whose great walls and hanging gardens were among the seven wonders of the world." Though apparently nothing further has been done, the idea of a rebuilt Babylon is in the minds of some!

Those Pesky Prophets

Two prophets of the Old Testament predicted the destruction of Babylon hundreds of years before it happened. Isaiah foresaw it this way:

> Your pomp and the music of your harps
> Have been brought down to Sheol;

Maggots are spread out . . . beneath you,
And worms are your covering.

Isaiah 14:11   NAS

Jeremiah described it in these phrases:

Encamp against her on every side,
Let there be no escape. . . .

. . . the desert creatures will live there along with the jackals.

I shall dispatch foreigners to Babylon that they may winnow her
And may devastate her land.

And Babylon will become a heap of ruins, a haunt of jackals,
. . . without inhabitants.

For the Lord is going to destroy Babylon. . . .

See Jeremiah 50:29, 39; 51:2, 37, 55   NAS

But Jeremiah adds a startling detail to this prophecy about the future of Babylon:

And it will never again be inhabited
Or dwelt in from generation to generation.
. . . so shall Babylon sink down and not rise again. . . .

Jeremiah 50:39; 51:64   NAS

So it would appear that Babylon will not be rebuilt (unless it be on a different site but using the same name), and we must look to some other city as the capital of world commerce.

The Other Candidate

The only other serious contender for the position is Rome. "Why Rome?" you say? Rome cannot be Babylon . . . or can it? In first-century thinking Rome was exactly that. The comparison of Rome to Babylon was common in Jewish literature, and this identification was adopted by the early Christians as well. The reason is simple: Old Testament Babylon stood for all that was against God, and New Testament Rome was the contemporary localization and embodiment of such evil.

When the apostle Peter wrote his first letter, the letter that we call First Peter, he said he was writing from "Babylon" (1 Peter 5:13).

This was understood to be a cryptic reference to Rome. Tertullian, who lived in the second century after Christ, wrote: "Babylon . . . is a figure of the city Rome, as being equally great and proud of her sway, and triumphant over the saints."

But Italy is virtually bankrupt. The government has had to borrow $17 billion from abroad just to stay afloat. How could Rome ever rise to be a center of world commerce? Yet a top official of one of Italy's nationalized industries predicts that Italy will become a great and rich world power in two or three years "because she sits astride the Mediterranean between Arab oil and an energy-starved Europe" (Alvin Toffler, "Beyond Depression," *Esquire,* February 1975, p. 134).

Regardless of where the capital will be located, Babylon is much more than an isolated city; it is a worldwide economic system.

The Tie That Binds

Economics is the name of the game, the tie that binds the world increasingly closer together. Bankers and politicians warn of "global recession" and "worldwide inflation." Thirteen nations that form the Organization of Petroleum Exporting Countries earned $112 billion from the rest of the world. But since they could not possibly spend it all, they ran up a surplus of $60 billion. The snowballing effects of the great oil price rise in 1974 added 3 or 4 percentage points to the U.S. inflation rate. Japan's inflation soared to 24 percent, due largely to her $18 billion bill for imported oil.

Poor countries were hurt the worst. In the developing nations, the extra expenditure for imported crude oil nearly equaled all of the foreign aid those countries received. India and Pakistan were typical. After paying their fuel bills, they had little money left to buy essential foods and fertilizers.

The snowballing cycle rolls on. Oil money is now being spent by OPEC nations to purchase banks and businesses in the industrial nations of the world. It has been estimated that OPEC could buy out all the companies listed on the New York Stock Exchange in 9.2 years, and all the companies on all major stock exchanges in the world in 15.6 years! Money talks we glibly say, but it will speak with thunderous volume as the end approaches.

Uranium, Too?

The shock of the oil crunch may be only the first of many shocks. Take uranium, for instance. "Other sources of energy must be found," we are warned. "Nuclear power will be an important part of the answer," we are told. But wait a minute. Look at what's happening, and see if the story sounds familiar.

In 1972 the raw material that is processed into nuclear fuel was selling for $6 to $8 a pound. There was virtually no profit in mining it. That same year an organization called the Uranium Producers Forum met in South Africa. From that time on buyers of uranium faced higher prices, with no competitive price cutting. In 1975 uranium was being offered for delivery in the mid-1980s at $24 a pound plus an annual escalator of about 7 percent.

But doesn't the United States have an almost unlimited supply of uranium? By no means. An official of the U.S. Atomic Energy Commission estimates that the United States will need to start importing uranium in 1979 or 1980. Breeder reactors won't have any significant impact on relieving that dependence on foreign uranium until the twenty-first century (*Forbes,* January 15, 1975, pp. 19–21).

Though the script may be rewritten in the years to come, the point of the drama is clear: The world is fast being welded into a single economic community.

So What's New?

But haven't there been severe economic crises before? And haven't we always survived?

Yes, there have been striking parallels to the current situation. Between January and September of 1919 the price of sugar rose 33 percent. The increasingly higher cost of living was the number one subject that year.

The United States and Mexico came close to war in 1919 over harassment of U.S. oil producers. The price of Pennsylvania crude doubled in a little over a year's time. High interest rates plagued the money market.

Yet by 1921 the price of oil had dropped and commodities had plunged 30 percent. Inflation had been replaced by deflation. Only after a severe economic shakedown was normalcy restored.

Yes, the scene has been acted out before. Only this time there are some vital differences in the situation. Worldwide interdependence between nations is the most significant factor. Economic isolation is nonexistent. Nations are no longer completely self-sufficient. The nations of the world today stand or fall together.

The Economic Forecast

Which will they do? Stand or fall? Both, the Bible predicts. The prophecy about Babylon in the eighteenth chapter of Revelation pictures a sudden and dramatic collapse of the world economic system.

(1) The collapse will be sudden. So sudden, in fact, that those who were actively engaged in its affairs one day, will see its collapse the next.

(2) The collapse will be complete.

> The music of harpists and musicians
>> flute-players and trumpeters,
>> will never be heard in you again.
> No workman of any trade
>> will ever be found in you again.
> The sound of a millstone
>> will never be heard in you again.
> The light of a lamp
>> will never shine in you again. . . .

Revelation 18:22, 23 NIV

(3) All the world will be affected. All nations will be enmeshed in the system, and the merchants of the whole world will feel the effects of the collapse.

(4) This will happen just before Jesus Christ returns to this earth to usher in His rule of justice.

Business As Usual

But the Bible also predicts that this sudden collapse will affect an economic system that flourishes and prospers right up to the end. In his vision the apostle John saw "business as usual" with merchants, ships, and sailors all engaged in worldwide trade. In spite of the tremendous trials of that future time of unprecedented trouble, there will also be great prosperity for some. Marketable items will include "gold, and silver, and precious stones, and pearls, and fine linens, and silk, and ivory vessels, and valuable pieces of wood, brass, iron and marble" (Revelation 18:12). Luxury and devastation will exist side by side.

Impossible? Not at all. Poverty and great wealth coexist in many countries today. The Via Veneto in bankrupt Italy is jammed with tourists and shoppers. While Detroit languished in the doldrums, unprecedented numbers of furloughed auto workers vacationed in Florida in the winter of 1974–75. And right to the end, the merchants of the world will apparently do a roaring last-days-of-Babylon business.

666

Just before the great collapse, Antichrist will use economics to promote his personal power. The increasing economic interdependence of nations will play right into his hands as he uses merchandising to tighten his grip on the world's population.

In order to identify his followers during the last years of the great tribulation period, Antichrist will line all people up and make them receive an identifying mark to show their allegiance to him. The mark will be placed on the forehead (if the person is unashamedly a supporter of Antichrist) or on the right hand (if he doesn't want it to be visible all the time). But to have the mark will be an economic necessity, for no one will be able to buy or sell unless he has Antichrist's identifying mark (Revelation 13:17).

In some special way the number 666 will be linked with Antichrist at that time. Just how, the Bible doesn't say. Perhaps that number will be the mark people receive, or at least one of the options they can choose. It will clearly identify them as followers of Antichrist.

And what of those who refuse? They will starve to death unless they have a friend or find a black market where they can buy food. Antichrist's personal cartel will mean hard times for those who resist.

How Does It All Add Up?

(1) Look for increasing economic interdependence between nations. Prices of raw materials will rise or fall, more or less in unison. The value of currencies will become more and more interrelated.

This, oddly enough, may represent an important factor in the formation of the political power blocs during the coming days of great tribulation. Political alliances may harden in order to protect economic interests. Economic needs in turn may promote the formation of alliances of nations. Antichrist, for example, may rise to a position of prominence, driven by economic forces. Some of the wars of those last days will undoubtedly be fought over economic goals. Nations will fight in order to gain strategic raw materials and strategically situated pieces of land. Economic pressures will play an increasing part in the political future of nations worldwide.

(2) Look for a shift in the centers of world wealth. Ultimately the capital of the Babylonian economy will not be Wall Street or London or Tokyo, but rather Rome or a city in the Middle East near ancient Babylon. Shifts in wealth may continue to be sudden and dramatic.

(3) Expect business trends to continue. Merchants will continue to conduct their affairs. Luxury items will be available for a luxury price. Ships will still ply the seas carrying materials and products to and from the nations of the world. Even traffic in drugs will be unabated (Revelation 18:23).

Any Advice?

What advice can this knowledge of the future give us about how to live in the present? For the follower of Christ, the apostle Paul gave a succinct summary statement: Be the kind of people who use this world but who do not abuse it (1 Corinthians 7:31). That simply means use every economic advantage (and disadvantage) to promote God's work in this world. Selfishness is wrong, in prosperity and in poverty. Generosity is right, regardless of the economic indicators.

But whatever may be in doubt about the future, one thing remains absolutely certain. Money cannot buy eternal life and peace with God; but Jesus Christ did. He paid the price for our alienation from God and now offers every individual the gift of life. And like any gift, it is free for the asking.

> The world and its desires pass away, but the man who does the will of God lives forever.
>
> 1 John 2:17 NIV

> For my Father's will is that everyone who looks to the Son and believes in him shall have eternal life. . . .
>
> John 6:40 NIV

13

The Best Is Yet to Come

> It came upon the midnight clear,
>> That glorious song of old,
> From angels bending near the earth,
>> To touch their harps of gold:
> "Peace on the earth, goodwill to men,
>> From heaven's all-gracious King:"
> The world in solemn stillness lay
>> To hear the angels sing.

So wrote Edmund Sears in that beautiful carol we sing at Christmastime. But as each Christmas rolls around, peace on earth seems more elusive. Can it ever be that the angels' promise to those humble shepherds will be fulfilled?

Christmas Day Every Day

We all know the feeling. In spite of the hustle and bustle of the season, there is the air of goodwill as Christmas approaches. People are a little more friendly; greetings become more common; wars enjoy cease-fires for a few days at Christmastime. We even like to leave the decorations up "just a little longer" to prolong the Christmas spirit.

One day that spirit will permeate the entire earth and never leave. Christmas speaks of Christ's presence, and when He returns it will be Christmas every day and everywhere.

Armageddon Is Not the End

Usually people use the word *Armageddon* to identify the end of the world. But Armageddon is not the end.

In the midst of the raging battle between East and West at Armageddon, Jesus Christ will return to the earth. He will defeat the armies of the nations, capture Antichrist and smash all who would seek to revolt against Him. Then, and only then, will earth's golden age begin.

Millennium

The English language has always used the word *millennium* to indicate a period of great happiness, and that is one of the meanings still found in the dictionary. But more precisely the word means a period lasting one thousand years and refers to a period of that duration during which Jesus Christ will rule on the earth. This will be earth's golden age.

But before King Jesus can reign, all opposition must be swept aside. Armageddon will demolish nearly all the forces of revolt, leaving but a single revolutionary on the earth. The one who started it all and who has led the rebels throughout history must yet be conquered before Christ's kingdom can come. And so as the birds of the skies are cleaning up the carnage of Armageddon, an angel will come from heaven to bind the devil and to confine him in the abyss for a thousand years (Revelation 20:2, 3). That will truly be a millennium—Jesus Christ as head of world government, and Satan totally inactive in the affairs of men. At long last will come the answer to the prayer Christ taught us to pray, "Thy kingdom come, thy will be done on earth as it is in heaven."

Although the catastrophes and judgments of that terrible time of tribulation will have radically changed the topography of the world, it is to this earth that the kingdom will come.

> And the Lord shall be king over all the earth: in that day shall there be one Lord, and his name one.
>
> Zechariah 14:9   KJV

Prophets on Target

Facts about the millennium are scattered throughout the Bible. Some have mistakenly thought that only the twentieth chapter of the last book of the Bible says anything at all about that period. In fact, many Old Testament prophets predicted numerous details about Christ's future world government. And, as usual, they were right on target. Everything they prophesied will happen exactly as predicted.

Jesus, too, talked about the coming golden age when He was here on earth the first time. On one occasion, when His disciples were complaining about their unrewarded labors, Jesus promised them a prominent place in the government of His coming kingdom (Matthew 19:28). Some of His parables emphasized His return (Luke 19:15;

Matthew 25:13, 19). Once again to the disciples He promised to return and "sit upon the throne of His glory," welcoming His followers into His kingdom (Matthew 25:31, 34). The best is yet to come!

I Wish . . . I Wish

Almost every human aspiration will be fulfilled in that coming kingdom. The things men have long dreamed of, planned and worked toward, and yet been unable to accomplish will at long last be realized. Peace, prosperity, longevity, justice, all the elusive longings of mankind, will be experienced by the citizens of Christ's kingdom.

No Watergate

How will this happen? What secret ingredient has been missing all these years? The answer: a righteous government, a government which combines positive justice with swift punishment of wrongdoers. The prophet Isaiah described the righteous King this way: "And righteousness shall be the girdle of his loins, and faithfulness the girdle of his waist" (11:5). No longer will courts need to depend on fallible witnesses who relate what they have seen or heard, for Christ will judge on the basis of His complete knowledge of all things. No cover-ups; no unpunished crimes; no miscarriages of justice.

Peace on Earth

The world seems to be staggering in a direction exactly opposite from the "peace on earth, goodwill toward men" about which the angels sang that first Christmas morning. Presidents and potentates all promise peace, but the dream evaporates before our very eyes. Why is this so? Simply because men think they can find peace apart from the Prince of Peace. They strive for peace between nations without first discovering the secret of peace within the human heart. Nations are only large groups of individuals. Until those individuals change, until we learn to live with our brothers in peace, it is folly to think of peace on the international level.

This does not mean that every subject of the kingdom will experience a changed heart. Those initially comprising the kingdom will all have changed hearts. But as children are born and grow up, some will gladly acknowledge the King and others will not. Those who rebel will nevertheless be obliged to obey the laws of righteousness established by the King. And because righteousness will reign, peace will follow.

Two prophecies in the Old Testament stand in stark contrast to each other. The first, by the little-known prophet Joel, pictures the dark days of the tribulation period just before Jesus Christ returns. In those days nations will "beat their plowshares into swords and their pruning hooks into spears" (Joel 3:10). But when King Jesus comes and takes the reins of government, exactly the opposite will come to pass. The well-known prophet Isaiah said: "They shall beat their swords into plowshares, and their spears into pruning hooks" (Isaiah 2:4). War before peace. Peace will ultimately come in the Person of the Prince of Peace.

United Nations

Man's United Nations will be torn apart by the warring power blocs of those days of tribulation. God's United Nations will replace it when Jesus comes again. Then, and only then, will there be one world government and one world Leader, with no rival purposes, no selfish interests, no injustice or inequity. Nations will no longer war against each other or strive for economic superiority, for Christ will rule a united world. Then, and only then, will the prophecy come true: "Nation shall not lift up sword against nation, neither shall they learn war any more" (Isaiah 2:4 KJV).

Think of the economic ramifications of this. The end of war will mean the end of expenditures for weapons. No need for maintaining balances of power between nations. Budgets will be drastically cut, tax rebates will abound (if there are any taxes at all in that utopian age). Fear will be dispelled. Costs of law enforcement will plummet. The position of Secretary of Defense will be totally eliminated!

Prosperity Plus

Peace on earth will also mean prosperity on earth. Isaiah saw it this way:

> The wilderness . . . shall be glad . . . and the desert shall rejoice, and blossom as the rose. It shall blossom abundantly, and rejoice even with joy and singing: the glory of Lebanon shall be given unto it, the excellency of Carmel and Sharon. . . .
>
> Isaiah 35:1, 2 KJV

Lebanon is known for its beauty; the word *Carmel* means "garden land" or "fruitful land"; and the excellency of Sharon refers to its dense vegetation cover and fertility. Each of the figures employed by Isaiah serves to underscore the productivity of the millennial kingdom.

This does not mean that people will get a "free ride." They will still work for a living, but their work will be rewarded beyond imagination. The prophet Amos described it this way: ". . . the plowman shall overtake the reaper, and the treader of grapes him that soweth seed" (Amos 9:13 KJV). In other words, one crop will follow on the heels of the other so closely that those who plow for the new crop will trip over those who are reaping the old one! Increased rainfall, increased number of crops, increased productivity, and unimaginable prosperity will characterize the age.

To Your Health, Too

Another of man's timeworn dreams, that of finding the fountain of youth, will also be realized in the millennium. Longevity will undergo such an increase that a 100-year-old person will be considered still a child (Isaiah 65:20). Everyone young and old will enjoy health as he has never known it before. Diseases will be arrested and cured. Blind eyes will see again and deaf ears will hear (Isaiah 35:5, 6). It is difficult to conceive of the heights of blessing man will enjoy during this golden age.

The Secret?

What's the secret again? The personal presence of the Lord. His law, which is absolutely right, will be the law of the world, and "the earth shall be full of the knowledge of the Lord, as the waters cover the sea" (Isaiah 11:9 KJV).

The Silent Minority

Strange as it may seem, not everybody will enjoy the new life-style imposed by a righteous government. Not all the citizens of the kingdom will appreciate justice. Some will even despise the King and loathe those who share in His government.

But because they live under a just rule, these rebels will either be obliged to conform or suffer the consequences. No one will be able to get away with violations of the law without paying the penalties, and the payments will be swift and sure. There will be no delays because of crowded court dockets; there will be no long trials while interminable arguments and appeals are raised; for Christ's judgments will flow from His perfect knowledge of all things.

Now, a thousand years is a long time. Even if your ancestors came to America on the Mayflower, their arrival was only 355 years ago. If we assume four generations every hundred years, then you could trace your ancestry back fourteen generations. But to trace your family back a *thousand* years would involve *forty* generations in your genealogical chart!

Think how many people can be born into one family during forty generations. No one knows how many individuals will survive those horrible years of trouble that will precede the kingdom, but these survivors will become the "kingdom settlers." They will of course have children, and their children will have children. With increased longevity and disease all but irradicated, the population will increase rapidly. Before a thousand years has elapsed, the earth will be fully replenished. And yet there will be no overpopulation problems, since increased productivity will easily sustain a large population.

Every single inhabitant of the world will have the opportunity to know the Lord and become one of His followers. Though all will have to obey His laws or suffer the consequences, yet He will not force anyone to give heart allegiance to Him. There will be many who, though outwardly conforming, will inwardly rebel. While the all-knowing King sees hearts, He will not punish that inward rebellion unless it erupts into open defiance of His rule.

Will We Ever Learn?

The millennial utopia ought to teach us something about ourselves. It will be a time of the greatest imaginable prosperity and blessing upon the world. Every dream that man has ever had will be fulfilled during that time. All the noble programs ever conceived to provide for the needs of mankind, programs which have been only partly successful today, will achieve full success during that golden age.

Most importantly, men will know the true religion, for the knowledge of the Lord will cover the earth.

And yet many will join the revolution against the King.

What do we learn from this? The point is simple but profound: Changing the world does not change the human heart. Even in the most ideal environment, corruption can exist within the heart. People need something more than environmental improvement and religious knowledge. They need new life that comes from a personal relationship with Jesus Christ. Many will experience that during the Kingdom, but some will reject the salvation offered by the King.

The Last Revolution

The seething undercurrent of rebellion will have one final chance to erupt at the conclusion of those thousand years. And erupt it will, for God will release Satan out of his prison to lead the last revolution.

Many will side with him, some having waited for decades, even centuries, for the opportunity to demonstrate their opposition to Christ and His government.

The apostle John described it this way: "And when the thousand years are expired, Satan shall be loosed out of his prison, And shall go out to deceive the nations which are in the four quarters of the earth . . . to gather them together to battle: the number of whom is as the sand of the sea. And they went up on the breadth of the earth, and compassed the camp of the saints about, and the beloved city . . ." (Revelation 20:7–9 KJV).

Satan's plot may be sketched something like this: After his release he will deceive some of the lesser officials of the Kingdom government. Apparently, many will respond favorably to his proposal to overthrow Christ. Secret cells and worldwide committees will be set up. Plans will be formulated, weapons clandestinely secured, armies formed. As the revolution gathers momentum, it will openly erupt in some part of the earth. The revolutionary forces will head for the capital city, Jerusalem, to strike at the very center of Christ's government. Along the way many citizens will hail the soldiers of Satan as deliverers and give them all the assistance they can. Success will seem to be within easy reach. The saints will appear to be outnumbered. Jerusalem will be surrounded. But just as the final attack begins, fire will come down from God out of heaven and devour the entire revolutionary army, reducing it to cinders. General Satan, stripped of his army, will be captured and cast forever into the lake of fire (Revelation 20:10).

Of course King Jesus does not have to permit this revolt to happen at all. He could stop it at any stage of its development. But He permits it to come to a climax in order to demonstrate conclusively that sin and rebellion will be punished; that no amount of intellectual knowledge, social betterment, or economic prosperity will ever change a rebellious human heart; and that the only way to change the heart of man is through Christ's gracious salvation.

But for those who follow the King, the best is yet to come.

The Living End

So we have come to the end—the end of time, that is. After describing Satan's crushing defeat, the apostle John saw a new heaven and new earth which will never end. He also saw a lake of fire which will never end. And he saw people who will live forever either in heaven or in that lake of fire.

Jesus Himself taught about hell and fire and eternal torment for those who reject Him (Mark 9:43, 44; Matthew 25:46). And Jesus' credentials as a prophet, you will recall, are impeccable. Many of His predictions have come to pass, assuring us and warning us that those yet unfulfilled will some day also come true.

It is sobering to realize that life does not end at the grave. Every soul born into this world will exist forever. Physical death is not cessation, but merely a separation, of body and soul. It is only temporary, for all will eventually be raised from the dead: some, in Jesus' words, "unto the resurrection of life" and some "unto the resurrection of damnation" (John 5:29 KJV).

There is no dead end, only a living end: endless existence in heaven or hell. Who decides the ultimate destiny? You do. Hear Jesus again:

Whoever puts his faith in the Son has eternal life, but whoever rejects the Son will not see that life, for God's wrath remains on him.

John 3:36 NIV

It Takes All Kinds

Jesus offered eternal life to any and all kinds of people. His message was uniform and His offer was universal.

Once a prominent religious leader named Nicodemus sought out Jesus in order to inquire about eternal life. Jesus did not discuss with Nicodemus their common heritage in Judaism. He did not explore areas of mutual agreement they might have had. He did not even dwell on the "good" in Nicodemus' religion. Rather, He said quite simply and clearly: "I tell you the truth, unless a man is born again he cannot see the kingdom of God" (John 3:3 NIV).

Nicodemus, though an expert in religion and a teacher of others, apparently did not understand that Jesus spoke of a spiritual rebirth, a supernatural work of grace resulting in a changed heart and life. So Jesus patiently explained, assuring Nicodemus that God loved him and wanted him in His family by faith. It was to this intellectual giant that Jesus spoke these familiar words: "For God so loved the world that he gave his one and only Son, that whoever believes in him shall not perish but have everlasting life" (John 3:16 NIV).

And what He said to Nicodemus is still true today.

A little later Jesus met someone at the opposite end of the social ladder, a woman whose life was so badly shattered that she seemed beyond help. She had three strikes against her. She was a woman, a Samaritan (and Samaritans were despised by Jews), and an adulteress. But Jesus, engaging her in conversation by a deep well to which she had come to draw water, offered her living water to cleanse her sinful heart. She didn't understand either, thinking that Jesus was offering her something to relieve her of those wearisome trips to the well. But He spoke plainly to her, telling of cleansing that gives eternal life (John 4:13):

> If you knew the gift of God and who it is that asks you for a drink, you would have asked him and he would have given you living water.

> John 4:10 NIV

Eternal life is a gift from the One who is the Lamb of God and takes away the sin of the world.

Perhaps you have read these pages with a skeptical eye. But before you dismiss what has been said, remember that God Himself stands behind the accuracy of these prophecies. Through His Son Jesus, and through His prophets and apostles of Old and New Testament times, He has relayed these predictions. And those messengers have passed the tests for true prophets. Above all, Jesus has proved Himself to be true, and thereby proved His claims to be valid.

But even if the messages of the prophets do not alert you, before finally dismissing them, take a good look again at current events. Were your parents or grandparents concerned about what went on in a tiny country in the Middle East called Israel? A generation ago Israel didn't even exist.

When before in the history of the United States have we ever been brought to our economic knees by the actions of a small group of nations, simply because they happened to be sitting on large reserves of oil?

Have you forgotten how recently the giant of the East has begun to shake himself, along with other emerging nations of the world?

Did colleges offer courses in witchcraft when you went to school?

How do you account for these unusual events converging in our present day?

Jesus said: "Even so, when you see all these things, you know that it is near, right at the door" (Matthew 24:33 NIV).

He also said: "Be ready, for the Son of Man will come at an hour when you do not expect Him" (Matthew 24:44).

Are you ready for the end? A living end?

53 – Ezek 38: 4, 15 –   horses !

57 – Ezek 39: 25, 26 –   God's mercy

54 – Ezek. 38: 12, 13 –   plundering

55 – Ezek 39: 10, 20 –   no fuel shortage